# WIN MORE
# SAILBOAT RACES

# WIN MORE

# SAILBOAT
# RACES

## C. STANLEY OGILVY

W. W. NORTON & COMPANY, INC., NEW YORK

The cooperation of the publishers of *Soundings* and *Yacht Racing* in providing many of the photographs is acknowledged with thanks.

Copyright © 1976 by W. W. Norton & Company, Inc.

First Edition

Library of Congress Cataloging in Publication Data
Ogilvy, Charles Stanley, 1913–
  Win more sailboat races.
  Includes index.
  1. Sailboat racing.  I. Title.
GV826.5.032  1976     797.1′4     75–38690
ISBN 0–393–03191–8

Published simultaneously in Canada
by George J. McLeod Limited, Toronto

Printed in the United States of America

1 2 3 4 5 6 7 8 9

# CONTENTS

"Some people look for lots of positive definitive answers, and want a book that tells them to put the jib leads at so-and-so many degrees and rake the mast X inches. But I think I get more out of books that are spiced with personal experiences and express a general racing philosophy or approach. I hope that over the years they help me avoid some of the serious mistakes that cost people regattas far more often than having the jib 7 millimeters too far in or out."

Peter Barrett

# PREFACE

The race was sailed on a fine, clear day, with an onshore breeze that gave just a little jump to the waves and allowed the whitecaps to show off their plumage against the blue of sea and sky. Your friend Joe, the average skipper, finished in the middle of the fleet, as usual; but when you asked him what kind of day he had, he replied, "Beautiful! Best race in weeks." And how did Moe, the fleet champion, answer the same question? With a black look he grumbled, "Terrible. We were on the wrong side of the shift and finished fifth"—or third, or whatever—but *not first,* and that ruined his day. He could hardly have told you whether the sun was shining. For him it wasn't.

It is the fashion today to lay enormous stress on the importance of *winning* yachting events. Writers of technical books and articles say, and not altogether in jest, "Winning isn't the most important thing, it's absolutely the only thing!" That may be true for them, but I cannot believe that it is true for all of us.

In your club's regular weekend racing fleet there are a few habitual winners, and then there is the rest of the fleet. The majority of skippers (and crews) are not big winners. They like racing for the sake of racing; otherwise why would they continue to turn up at the starting line time after time? They seldom finish first and yet they keep coming back for more. They are able, but not expert. They would like to do better, and are eager to find out how to improve their performance level; but it is not for them a matter of life or death.

I do not mean that this book should be called "How to Win Races Without Really Trying." You have to try, and try hard. But it is not necessary to work yourself into a state of nerves over it. You can have good, keen racing and still maintain a sane balance between relaxation and enthusiasm, between casualness on the one hand and hypertension on the other. I think you can raise your score and your spirits at the same time.

A friend who enjoys putting me on picked up an earlier book of mine and glancing at the price, said, "Hmm! That works out at about a nickel a page." When he adopts this tone I know that more is to follow. "Some pages aren't worth a nickel; some are worth maybe eight cents."

That's about the size of it. You should read all the racing books you can get your hands on, even if you don't agree with everything they have to offer. There are sure to be helpful nuggets here and there that you don't want to miss. I offer you this book in that spirit. It won't work miracles for you; no book can do that. But if it helps you even a little; if it makes your racing afternoons less frustrating; if, by analyzing the problems, it points the way toward solving them; and above all, if it allows you to get more enjoyment out of racing—then you will be that much the gainer.

Let's hope that there will be some pages worth, one way or another, a lot more than eight cents.

# WIN MORE
# SAILBOAT RACES

# [I]
# YACHT RACING FOR THE ORDINARY MORTAL

Before the Second World War the good books on yacht racing could be counted on one hand—in fact, on one finger: Manfred Curry's *Yacht Racing; The Aerodynamics of Sails and Racing Tactics,* first published by Charles Scribner's Sons, N.Y., in 1928, fifth edition in 1948. This book, now somewhat dated, has been followed by others by the same author and revisions by other authors; nevertheless there is so much of value in the original volume that it is well worth looking into. Many libraries have it. My copy is dog-eared from much re-reading. Regardless of details, its whole approach, the philosophy of the book, makes good sense. One notes in particular the recurrent emphasis on natural phenomena: What can we learn from nature that will improve our sailing?

After the war the sport of small-boat racing changed rapidly from the pastime of the few to the passion of a very large number of people. New books began to appear; today many are available, and more turn up all the time. They are all written by the big names of the sport, the superskippers, and they all tend to leave one gasping. You finish such a book exhausted, muttering, "How could I ever stand the pace?" Is it unfair to say that some of these experts tell us too little about how to improve our performance and too much about how good theirs is? Everybody already knows that they are great; what you and I are more interested in is how to get some of this greatness to rub off on us. One good skipper of my acquaintance sails on a small lake in a fleet of boats that happens to be of an Olympic class. After having read a specialized article on tuning for that class he shook his head. "How can I understand what he's trying to say? In our fleet we don't even have most of those fittings on the boats, and I wouldn't know what to

HOWEY CAUFMAN

I agree, sir; it looks like a clumsy piece of equipment.

do with them if we did have them." Yet that fleet enjoys keen racing among equally matched boats.

There has been a "hardware explosion" that has created great turmoil in some fleets and caused others to break up entirely. When the top skippers change the rig every year in order to incorporate new devices and inventions, and when it seems to be necessary to do the same in order to remain competitive with them, many owners become disenchanted and quit the class. Note that I say *seems* to be necessary, because one is never sure how much of winning is due to new gadgets and how much to superior skill. There is always the nagging thought, "He may have beaten us because his boat is faster, and therefore we should rebuild our rig so that we have everything he has." The trouble is, even if we do, next year he will probably come out with more new apparatus. I am not saying that this is necessarily bad; but it is a game that not everyone likes to play. In its extreme form, fortunately, it does not apply to most fleets. It certainly does apply at the highest level of international competition, but that is a level, to borrow a phrase from academic jargon, "beyond the scope of this text."

Most sports are extremely athletic; they can be pursued successfully only by the young and strong. One of the great attractions of sailboat racing is that you can continue to enjoy it into middle life and beyond, even if you are putting on weight in the wrong places, provided that you keep reason-

**Spectacular, but is it worth it?**

AL AUDLEMAN, GULF YACHTING

ably fit and mentally alert. Manfred Curry had remarkable insight for a youngster. When he was eighteen he wrote,

> "No other sport requires such versatility of talent and accomplishment as sailing a race: Logical thinking; clear, quick consideration; presence of mind; courage; endurance, often for hours at a time; keenness of observation; delicacy of feeling. To these may be added as desirable, though not absolutely essential, physical strength, agility and a certain feeling for equilibrium."

The modern treatises are written by the young athletes who sail the so-called high-performance boats. To my mind the performance of a boat depends on the ability of the people in the cockpit; but let that pass. The term "high performance" has become more or less synonymous with acrobatics and feats of physical endurance on the part of skipper and crew. To the top skippers in the Olympic and similar classes, racing is at least in part an athletic contest. That is not what racing means to most of us. We are out there because sailing is an enjoyable occupation. When it ceases to be enjoyable, something is wrong somewhere. One authority even writes of the *pain* of good crewing. He expects his crew to be willing to undergo nothing short of physical torture. My opinion on that sort of approach to the sport we love is unprintable. I cannot believe that winning (and there is no other reward) is that important. If it is that important for the few, they can have it. The vast majority of us do not want to be told that we have to practice back-bending exercises on the edge of the bathtub all winter in order to get "in training" for hiking. We just want to go out there and race.

And so we get back to *you,* Mr. Average Good Skipper. You do not have a legacy to spend on a new boat and equipment, you do not have trained athletes for crews, you race mostly in local waters, without Olympic aspirations but for the sheer pleasure of the game. Can anything be done to improve your racing results? I think that the answer is yes. There are many ways to help bring you to a high position on the score sheet without breaking your back or your bank account.

The purpose of this book is to investigate some of these possibilities.

# [2]
# CONDITIONING
# THE HULL

If a skipper tells me that his boat just won't go, especially down-wind, my first recommendation is that he haul her out and take a good long look at the bottom. It is surprising how many skippers try to get through a racing season with a bottom that is in poor shape and getting worse each day. The bottom of the keel in particular is usually in disgraceful condition.

Most of this book will deal with problems and situations that can be handled by a suitable application of intelligence and ingenuity. This chapter is an exception. A bad bottom cannot be cured by thinking about it. Nor can the situation be remedied in five minutes. Obtaining a good racing finish is a project for the winter months. The bottom (and I mean *all the underbody*) must be sanded and filled until it is smooth. As it moves through the water the hull drags a layer, or layers, of water with it, causing (1) friction between the hull and the layers and (2) turbulence as the layers break up and re-form. Both friction and turbulence can be reduced, although never eliminated, by a smooth finish. Physicists tell us that for "perfect" flow the finish would have to be optically smooth, which means the kind of finish on the surface of an instrument's lens; far smoother than anything attainable with sandpaper, however fine. C. A. Marchaj says that a surface sufficiently smooth to maintain satisfactory laminar flow as opposed to turbulent flow must have "practically no roughness detectable to finger tips" (*Skin Friction Drag on Yachts and its Reduction,* from Lands' End Yachtsman's Equipment Guide for 1968). He goes on to say that the surface should be like that of a concert piano, but not necessarily shiny. Permissible roughness is then calculated as 1.6 mils, which means that a bump or crack must not be more

HARRY MONAHAN

These 5.5 Metres follow the older style of rudder attached to the keel. Note the superb racing finish on *Luv*. The absence of any stripe at the waterline is alleged to confuse the competition by not revealing the angle of heel.

than 1.6 thousandths of an inch above or below the rest of the surface. I have no way of measuring such minute roughnesses, but my guess is that 1.6 mils is considerably less than detectable to finger tips.

The most nearly ideal finish obtainable today would appear to be what comes on a new fiberglass hull. If you have just acquired a new boat, by all means sail "on the gel coat" as long as possible. If you so much as touch the bottom with cleansing powder, rubbing compound, or sandpaper, whether to remove fouling or for any other reason, you have marred that wonderfully smooth gel coat and can never quite get it back. Once that happens you have to take other steps to make the finish as smooth as possible. That usually means filling and sanding, filling and sanding, until you are satisfied. I am almost never satisfied. My neighbor asks, "Don't you ever finish that job?" Well, no, not entirely. And as a result the boat's racing bottom is gradually improving all the time, instead of deteriorating.

There are critical spots on the hull that nearly always need attention. One of these is the bottom of the keel. Turn the boat over and fix it. If your boat is too big for that, the chances are that the boat usually sits in the same position on its cradle or trailer, so that there are places, perhaps the whole bottom of the keel, that are always inaccessible. This will never do. You might be able to rig a chain hoist from a beam or a large tree and lift the boat during the winter. If that is impossible, hang the hull on the club hoist some winter weekend and work on the bottom of the keel there.

Another place difficult to keep even relatively smooth is the gap between the rudder post and the skeg, or whatever the rudder is attached to. The open space there creates permanent turbulence, a real problem. Try

Hung up to condition the bottom of the keel.

to keep this space small so that the transition from skeg to rudder is as fair as possible. The water has to work its way past the whole hull, not only the parts that are easiest to take care of. You may have heard it argued that the rudder is in the wake of the keel where there is so much turbulence anyway that there is no point in trying to correct a small part of it. Those who hold that view would do well to consult the designer of a certain unsuccessful 1974 contender for the defense of the America's Cup. I daresay he has altered his opinion about that.

For many people wood is esthetically more pleasing to look at and work with than fiberglass. But I am afraid that the small wooden racing boat is a thing of the past. A quip current just a few years ago is already outdated: "If God had intended us to build fiberglass boats, he would have given us fiberglass trees!" Glass is here to stay, at least until some better material comes along. When the older generation of boat builders passes on—and they are nearly all gone—their art will die with them. There may never again be people trained to construct boats out of wood.

In 1976, however, there are plenty of wood boats still racing, and you may own one of them. If you do, your patching procedure is different from that of the glass-boat owner. Probably one of the filled epoxies is your best bet for cracks and gouges in the wood. Don't use a fiberglass product that will be harder than the surrounding wood. Even epoxy is difficult to sand smooth without cutting into the wood. For small nicks and cracks, or temporary filling jobs, ordinary lacquer-base automotive glazing putty is quite serviceable. It dries fast, is easy to apply, and holds up even under water for weeks if built up with thin coats. The drain plug in my boat is removed only in the winter, and is smoothed over and sealed each spring with automotive putty. This is much softer than the epoxies and "poly"-fillers, and allows the plug to be taken out in the fall without blasting powder.

For major repair jobs, especially on the lead keel, I have had some success with a product called *Rez-Zin* (Marson Co., Chelsea, Mass.), which is essentially filled fiberglass resin without the glass cloth. It is a putty that must be mixed (carefully!) with a few drops of catalyst, and has an extremely short working time before hardening, but it sands nicely and is exceedingly adhesive. If a rock has had the bad manners to get in the way of your keel and left you with a sizable dent to fill, Rez-Zin may be the answer.

When smoothing any part of the underbody of the boat you must keep in mind two things. The first is to get rid of the small irregularities and roughnesses, scratches, and bumps that can be eliminated by sanding and filling. This is the easy part: the water, in passing over the hull, flows best over surfaces that are as smooth as possible to the touch. But there is a second consideration, and that is the designer's lines. No racing boat has wavy lines, that is, surfaces that show even slight concavities or mounds. It is generally conceded that this *fairness* of the hull, or smoothness "in the large," must be maintained. That is accomplished by eliminating—or never introducing—any slight but long hills and valleys. These are harder to detect and to correct than the tiny ones. You must guard against creating a hollow by overzealous sanding of a small area. Sand only with a large block, never with the fingers. It's harder work, and seems to go slower; but the hull or keel will not remain fair unless you sand by hand with a block. A power sander is not recommended, except possibly a small vibrator handled with extreme care. Rotary and belt sanders are much too powerful and could ruin the surface in seconds.

When you think you have finished fairing the keel or centerboard or rudder, give it the flashlight test. This is the ultimate bump detector; you may be disagreeably surprised by how much it reveals. Put the flashlight close up to the surface, at night, with the beam directed parallel to the surface. Shadows will show up in the hollows, and you can decide whether you must sand some more. If the decision is Yes, then the sanding block must be large enough to take down the tops of the hills and jump across the valleys. If the surface is convex, like the bottom of a dinghy, it may be necessary to devise a curved block. Hard rubber is good, or perhaps the sandpaper can be fastened with staples to a large flexible batten.

Fiberglass boats, though in many ways easier to take care of than wood boats, are by no means completely maintenance free. The topsides, particularly around the rail, get chipped and dented whenever you run into something or something runs into you. Bad breaks in the fiberglass or actual holes in the hull should be repaired professionally. Little scars in the gel coat or nicks in the rail you can fix yourself. Matching the color of the fiberglass is a problem, even if it is white. No mender that I can find is as white as the glass itself. Real gel coat would do the trick, if you know how to use it: I don't, and succeed only in making an unholy mess if I try.

Do your best to keep anything from hitting the side of your boat. Some of us who were brought up in cedar hulls dentable at the slightest touch have carried along the notion that we ought to be kind to our glass hulls too. But other people, especially youngsters who never had wood-boat training, seem to think that nothing can hurt glass. They are seriously mistaken. Even slight impact with a heavy object, like another boat, although seeming to leave the hull intact, will in fact scar the gel coat with many minute cracks that radiate in a star from the point of contact. These cracks, invisible at first, show up under weathering and continue to get worse. The only way to eliminate them is to prevent their occurrence in the first place.

The condition of the topsides may not have much effect on boat speed. Nevertheless no one likes to sail a sloppy-looking boat, and her appearance is worth caring for both for psychological reasons and to protect the value of your investment. Fiberglass, if left to itself in the sun and weather, dulls and discolors with age. This aging can be much slowed by inside winter storage if you are so fortunate as to have that available. My boat stays outside, without a wraparound cover, and I have had good luck in keeping the surface bright by a judicious use of fiberglass polish. During the summer I don't put anything on the topsides; but in the fall a coat of polish is applied above the waterline wherever the sides are exposed to sun and rain, that is, all places not protected by the winter cover. By springtime the polish has hardened and requires some elbow grease to get it off; but the result is a bright, shiny, new-looking finish.

Of far greater importance than the sides is the racing bottom. Once you have got it smooth, or if the boat is new, how to keep it that way? If you are sailing on the gel coat in salt water and your class rules allow only occasional haulouts, one solution is a "bird bath," a plastic pool with buoyant edges enclosing the boat at the mooring. These are not cheap, and it is a nuisance getting the boat in and out, but they work. It is surprising what a few chlorine pellets do to the marine life.

A different attack is lots of swimming. I swim around my boat at least twice a week, usually more often. If you don't relish twenty minutes in cold water, get yourself a wet-suit: it really does keep you warm, and provides about the right amount of buoyancy for relaxed swimming. The more frequently you clean the bottom, the easier the job. Baby barnacles two or three days old wipe off at a touch, but if you leave them long enough to get a firm grip they are the very devil to remove. The point is that they must be wiped or rubbed off with your hand; I use a soft cotton glove. As soon as they have to be scrubbed or sanded off, there goes your gel finish, once and for all.

The original gloss of the gel coat is long gone from the *Flame,* because I made the initial mistake of painting the bottom. At that time I had just

The Etchells-22 has the rudder hung on a small skeg.

come from many years of sailing Stars, which are kept out of water, and not knowing much about antifouling paint I thought it would be nice to try it. I still don't know much about it, but I do know one thing: no paint that I ever saw or heard of is nonfouling to the extent that it completely prevents marine growth. Antifouling paint is much better than nothing, of course, and it inhibits and slows the growth, but the finish requires attention just the same. A fresh coat of soft bronze or copper carrier is perhaps as close to nonfoulable as you can get; but this is not satisfactory for a boat that is to be seriously raced, because it is too soft and too rough. Therefore you sand and polish it, and there goes half the antifouling quality; so you have to swim anyway. On the *Flame* we ended up with a bronze bottom that had not seen fresh paint for three years and was polished so smooth that it had virtually no antifouling left. Last summer we took it all off and are now back to the (dulled) gel coat. I hope Marchaj is right with his "smooth but not necessarily shiny."

Fashions in bottom paints come and go. Just a few years ago the black graphite-filled paints were popular. By 1975 there had been a swing in some quarters to Woolsey's Blue Streak Vinylast, a copper-filled antifouling paint that, like the graphite products, is alleged to have built-in go-fast properties. Whether it really does I cannot say; but I do know that it is easy to apply, adheres well, and can be wet-sanded to a fine smooth finish. Blue Streak seems to be less temperamental than some of the other paints; that is, it can be applied over most well-prepared surfaces without developing the usual blisters after a few days or weeks of submersion. If it requires any thinning, be very sure to use *only* the specified thinner.

A nearly perfect solution to the fouling problem has recently been developed by the fiberglass industry: a surface with a marine-growth inhibitor built into it. The gel coat looks no different from the regular kind, but it stays clean, or almost clean, in salt water. Eventually the antifouling leaches out and disappears, and it is too soon to say exactly when this happens. It is known to work for at least one season and into the second. The only boat in our fleet that has it is now in its third season, and the owner tells me that he does have to clean the bottom, but far less frequently than the rest of us. A somewhat costly extra, and not even guaranteed by builders, it would nevertheless seem to be worth a try.

Towing tests have indicated that a slightly slimy hull moves through the water more easily than a freshly launched clean hull. Nature confirms this: fish have a light slime finish. Nor is it just slime from the water. A fish does not acquire barnacles. Nature has evolved for the fish a 100 percent antifouling surface that moves through the water with minimum effort. Do not worry, however, that your boat will have too little slime on it. It will have too much all too soon. An optimum amount will probably be there (in warm water) within twenty-four hours of launching.

If a hull has a rough bottom you might think it should retard the boat by X miles per hour whether upwind or down. But it turns out that X is not a constant. A smooth bottom is only one of many factors contributing to the speed of the boat. Trim, tune, and helmsmanship are of major importance upwind, probably less so downwind. Wind resistance, especially of the mast and rigging, is a strong retarding force upwind that actually turns into an assist off the wind. The ability to steer the boat through the seas is an art that is of major consequence upwind. Downwind, on the other hand, the boat is not slamming into the waves but gliding over them. The helm still needs guidance, but that guidance is not as delicate nor as critical. Pitching moments, lightness of the rig aloft, etc., have little effect downwind. Windshifts are so important on the windward leg that they may (usually do) decide the whole race. But even disregarding windshifts, because we are talking about boat speed, I am suggesting that there is a whole set of forces tending to slow the boat on the windward leg, of which skin friction is only one. Downwind most of these disappear or are minimized, leaving the *percentage* of the retarding due to skin friction much higher than it was upwind. That is why a reduction in the skin friction is so much more noticeable off the wind. Just for the sake of some figures, purely hypothetical and not based on any experimental data, suppose that the skin friction contributed 5 percent of the total retarding forces upwind and 25 percent of the total retarding forces downwind under the same wind and sea conditions. If that were so, whatever improvement you could make in the hull surface would be five times as effective downwind as upwind.

In some classes there are tolerances on the section shapes of keel or centerboard, rudder, and skeg. By this I mean the shape of horizontal cross-section at any given depth. If you are allowed to shape your rudder or keel for optimum performance, again be guided by the fish. Nature has not designed (or evolved) many fish with sharp noses. A well-designed modern keel looks something like the cross section of a trout or bass: blunt forward, widest point slightly forward of amidships, then tapering to a very fine trailing edge. Fish have various forms of leading edge, but there is no nonsense aft: always the fins and tail (rudder) trail away to a knife-edge. We cannot do as well with the appendages on our boats, but we can aim in that direction. The finest practicable trailing edge is the best.

The leading edge should certainly not be sharp. It should probably be rounded to the maximum allowable radius; but there is a limit. According to Marchaj, the bluntness can be overdone. Figure 1 and the accompanying commentary are reproduced from the previously mentioned 1968 Lands' End article. These equipment guides, published annually by Lands' End, Chicago, Illinois, always carry a few feature articles containing much food for thought in addition to the catalogue of merchandise.

It is interesting to note that Manfred Curry recommended almost the same section shape for a keel nearly fifty years ago.

**Figure 1**

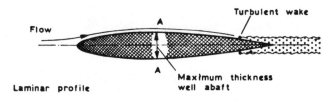

Laminar profile

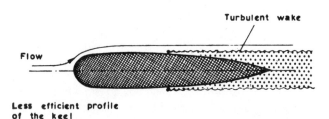

Less efficient profile
of the keel

The significance of the shape of the keel proper tends to be rather underestimated, perhaps because the underwater part of the hull is not as conspicuous as sails are.

The action of the keel as a hydrofoil is still a "grey area" and it is most probable that further progress towards better performance when sailing to windward might be facilitated by investigating the secrets of keel efficiency. The importance of the keel proper is certainly no less than that of the sails.

Most of the reconditioning and improvements described in this chapter can be accomplished during the winter months when the boat is readily available in your basement or garage. But if the boat has to be stored in a place that cannot be warmed even temporarily, then use of some of the "poly"-menders and paints is restricted to warm weather. Check the label for temperature requirements. It may be possible to apply a catalyst-operated filler below the recommended temperature, but it will take hours or days instead of minutes to harden and cure. Heat applied locally is one solution. If you are repairing a small damaged area in cold weather a single floodlight bulb turned on the new work from a distance of a foot or two does wonders.

# [3]
# GEAR AND EQUIPMENT

A recent book by a big-time champion lays great stress on the importance of getting rid of extra weight. The reader is advised to shorten all extra length of rope ends, to go around under the deck with wire-cutter and hacksaw and cut off the ends of protruding bolts, even to maintain a slippery deck so that the water can run off it more quickly. While these measures may be a bit extreme, it is true that you should not carry around a lot of useless junk, especially since it has a way of accumulating in the ends. If something is in the way the tendency is to toss it up forward (or far aft), where it is forgotten; and the ends of the boat are exactly the places that should be the lightest.

Clean out all lockers and hiding places frequently and take ashore everything you don't actually use except for an irreducible minimum of spare parts. On a small boat these spares are limited to a few bolts and shackles and maybe a jib block on a slide. If anything really major lets go you can't fix it during the race anyway. It is not possible to carry aboard a small day sailer the kind of floating machine shop that is indispensable on a long ocean race, so don't try.

Whether to carry a spare spinnaker pole is a borderline question. For many years we didn't, and then one day when the end fitting broke off the pole we wished we had a spare. The crew managed to hook the pole to the mast somehow and, as usual, saved the day. After that we carried a spare pole—and of course never had another emergency. It weighs six pounds, and I have about concluded that it should be left ashore again.

There are a few major principles that have more to do with keeping the rig in the boat than with sailing speed. Most dismast-

The Dragon Class rules require that the lower spreaders be permanently fastened horizontally, resulting in a bad angle with the shroud. Compare Figure 2.

15

ings are the result of rigging failure. Sometimes the failure is intrinsic: a turnbuckle or a tru-loc lets go and the mast instantly goes over the side. Nothing much can be done about that kind of disaster. There is no method that I know of to detect in advance a flaw in a casting or a cold-rolling.

Dismastings from any other cause, however, are at least partly the fault of the skipper, and often could have been prevented. A spreader may buckle or tear out of its socket; but why? The spreader was properly designed, and is doing its job on other boats; why did it fail on this one? Obviously because it was being overstressed, overloaded in a direction never intended to bear a load. Spreaders are pure compression members and should not be expected to withstand twisting or bending forces. If the rig is in balance it should stay in one piece.. In order not to have any tendency to bend up or down, a spreader should exactly bisect the angle made by the stay that passes over its outer end. In Figure 2, the two angles marked *a* must be equal to each other and the two angles marked *b* must be equal to each other. The forces trying to tear the spreaders off in a horizonal direction (fore and aft) are a bit more difficult to counteract. If the mast is carried perfectly straight there is no problem: just lead the stay from the outer end of the spreader to a point on the chainplate opposite the center of the mast. When the mast is bowed aft, however, as it often is nowadays, the spreader is pulled back and must be given a counterpull

**Figure 2**

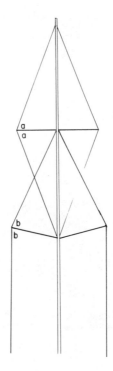

forward by attaching the stay farther forward on the chainplate. The mast is under heavy compression lengthwise, and once it begins to bend that bend wants to increase. That is why the main lower should lead aft, as a preventer, probably to the farthest aft hole on the chainplate.

The spreaders and spreader clips should be inspected frequently for signs of fatigue or the beginning of cracks in the metal. At the slightest indication that such a break is developing, renew the whole fitting immediately, and try to analyze the cause of the strain. Something is probably out of balance and should be corrected. Be sure, for instance, that the mast is seated perfectly straight in the mast step. If it is only a few degrees out of true (twisted), trouble may be in store. Check all openings in the spar where sheaves have been installed. Aluminum is very weak in shear, and once the tiniest tear develops in the metal wall of the spar itself it will quickly grow under stress.

Check frequently all parts of the gooseneck fitting and the boom itself. A broken boom will not cause the rig to fall out of the boat, but it will lose the race for you. Booms and goosenecks break because of the heavy load applied by the vang. I try to design my vang to contain a point of weakness, so that in the event of an overload the vang itself will let go before the boom breaks. It's easier to fix, and much cheaper! An almost guaranteed way to break a boom is to trip it heavily in the water when you broach on a fast beam reach. Either don't vang down when there is risk of broaching, or station a man with the vang line in his hand for instant emergency release.

It is important to keep everything aloft as light and streamlined as possible. Wind resistance not only holds back the boat directly but also interferes with the proper flow of air onto the sails. The construction of the mast and rigging is a perpetual compromise between desirable lightness and adequate strength. Everything must hold together, but it must also be as smooth and as light as your class rules allow.

Extra weight is especially harmful aloft because of the unnecessary moments created. Every time the boat pitches on even a small wave the mast has to be swung through a long arc fore and aft. It requires substantial forces to start and stop this motion; these forces interfere with the easy motion of the boat over the waves and correspondingly slow her progress through the water. If you don't believe there is a heavy pitching moment at the masthead, go up there some rough day. You won't try it twice.

For exactly the same reason the ends of the boat should be kept light. Get in the habit of storing spare gear and equipment amidships (but don't put the tool box too near the compass). Especially don't store the anchor forward, or aft. Remove those heavy bronze bow chocks and replace with at most one small aluminum chock. Take the mooring cleat off the foredeck; you can just as easily tie up or tow from the mast, and the foredeck man will bless you for getting rid of something he was always stumbling over.

A paddle is part of the required equipment in most classes. There is on the market a fiberglass-and-aluminum device with a paddle blade at one end and two hooks at the handle end. These hooks are supposed to help you retrieve the spinnaker sheet if it gets caught above and outside the main boom. The best place for the whole contraption is at the bottom of the bay.

In the first place the paddle blade is not strong enough; ours broke across the middle in ordinary use. Furthermore, any device for pushing the spinnaker sheet around the boom is a loser: the sheet has too much tension on it in any kind of breeze. The main point is that it is not necessary. If the sheet has climbed up the leech of the mainsail and you don't like it there, just release the vang momentarily; a crew member now goes aft until he can reach the spinnaker sheet and tuck it under the main boom, which you trim in for him if he has trouble. The job is accomplished in a jiffy on any modern short-boomed boat, without any patented pushers or pullers.

Now you have to find yourself a nice light old-fashioned wooden canoe paddle, not easy to come by; but I leave that to you.

We stow the spinnaker pole amidships and low down, not slung underneath the deck. In fact I don't like anything, not even lines, hanging on

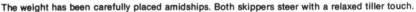

**The weight has been carefully placed amidships. Both skippers steer with a relaxed tiller touch.**

hooks. Anything hanging swings and sways and creates unnecessary moments of its own, however small. Even the crew should come solidly to roost. In our boat when weather conditions call for live ballast inside, they like to "sit on their heels" in order to see out of the deep cockpit. This won't do: it is a very unstable position. Make them plant their weight firmly on their rear ends, as low down as possible. Going to windward the skipper and crew should be grouped close together in the fore and aft direction, again to keep the weight out of the ends.

Good skippers and crews are always mulling over ways of improving the boat's running gear and fittings, to make them more efficient and easier to work with. I confess that I have probably dragged my feet in the game of refitting an Etchells-22. Not being a great gadgeteer, I prefer simplicity to complication, provided the simpler arrangement accomplishes the task smoothly. This approach is all right if you don't overdo it. If a fitting is clumsy or in the wrong place, don't live with it: move it to the right place or get rid of it. Listen to your crew. Sometimes their suggestions won't work, but often enough they will. Anyway they may be worth trying; you can always go back to the old system if necessary.

To be specific: It took about four replacements, using a different make each time, before we got a mainsheet cam cleat that would really hold without grabbing so tight that it was impossible to release in a hurry. The second season we had the boat we devised a better way of fastening (locking) the jib halyard, and I have now designed a third way. The crew didn't like one (central) jib winch so we went to two. When I changed the mainsheet blocks to modern ball-bearing affairs, I discovered the first day something that I should have predicted. The old simple blocks had enough internal friction to act as a slight brake when the sheet was being eased. The new aristocratic ones have so little friction that they run *too* freely. You need an assist on the last block, a ratchet action that acts as a snubbing winch. The complete system with optional ratchet works like a dream, and I am sure that any skipper who has one will smile at my ignorance in only recently finding out about it.

Most people prefer to be able to take the main traveler car to windward of amidships for certain conditions of wind and water. This requires traveler-control tackle that probably didn't come with the boat. There are as many different arrangements as there are skippers. I have yet to learn of an automatic way of shifting the traveler car to windward on each new tack. If you can devise a self-shifting scheme, please let me in on it. The middle man does it on our boat, if he remembers. On large yachts the traveler is often located just forward of the helmsman, who adjusts the tackle because he can hardly forget something two feet in front of his face. But that isn't the answer. The helmsman should steer, and think, and have an absolute minimum of other duties.

If the backstay is an important adjustment on your boat, the cleat of the backstay tackle must be in a readily accessible position. Does the out-haul operate as smoothly as it should? The vang is a perpetual problem. Look at the vang systems being used by other people in your class and adopt the one you think might be the best. Make the major changes during the winter months when you have time to work them out and to manu-facture the necessary new fittings, but don't postpone small changes if they will do any good. My notes during a busy race week read: "Thursday morning moved the jib leads two inches inboard, which seems to be about right. Yesterday rebuilt the gooseneck fitting so that the boom can be locked partway up the slide on a run. The old main didn't need that, but it is a definite improvement with the new sail."

A good compass is more than worth the difference in price over an inferior one. If you need a compass on each side of the boat, be sure to get a matched pair, by which I mean two that read alike. If a single compass is 5° off uniformly on all headings you can get used to it and make the necessary allowance; but if your two compasses read 5° apart, all your tacking calculations are thrown out of whack. I was aboard a racing boat not long ago where the two compasses differed by 15°. It is hardly neces-sary to report that that boat is not winning many prizes.

Before the start of each race, as soon as our course is posted, we look up the compass headings of all the legs and write them down on the deck in (easily erasable) pencil. This has the dual advantage of providing a written record of the course letters. (Oh, yes, it's entirely possible to for-get the course; we've done that too. I doubt very much whether you could name an old mistake or invent a new one that we haven't made on the *Flame.*) It is also a good idea before the start to harden on the wind and note the compass headings you get on both tacks, for future reference when you are concerned with windshifts. This is one reason for matching compasses: if they differ they will give you a false reading on the number of degrees through which you can tack.

Some boats have so much adjustable gear, so many "strings and pul-leys," that the entire space under the deck is a maze of apparatus. On a boat where the people disappear somewhere over the side or live six feet out on a trapeze, this may be necessary. Everything has to be double-ended and on a high mechanical advantage. But if you don't need a bunch of reels, winches, and tackles, don't install them. A ten-to-one mechanical advantage may sound nice but it has many drawbacks. It comes in easily but won't go out, often requiring shock cord (an added accessory) to pull it out. You end up with a string in your hand ten times as long as the distance through which the business end has to move. Double-ended lines have a way of working through so that when you want to ease your end you find that there is none left. An auxiliary gadget must be incorporated to prevent that. Complication leads to complication. Boats fitted out in this

This may not be as bad as it looks; maybe only a few stubborn rubber bands have to break.

fashion may be a necessary part of life for the superchampion of a high-development Olympic class, but they are not for you and me.

Change the things that are inconvenient or awkward, but do it judiciously. Keep the boat simple and workable. There are better ways to win races than by trying to devise superior gadgets.

The preliminaries are over and we have finally arrived at the starting line. The chips are down; the real game is about to begin. Owen C. Torrey, whose skill as a sailmaker is matched by his sagacity and wit with a pen, puts it well. He is referring to the rating yachts, the big ocean racers for which people spend money into six figures just to get a faster boat. Even so he writes:

> "It is belaboring the obvious to say that boats and equipment don't win yacht races; people win yacht races. Everyone admits that and then proceeds to behave as if it weren't true. The technology of sailing is substantial and becoming more so every year, but the fact remains that yacht racing is an athletic contest and the prizes are won by the skillful.
>
> "That being so, it would seem that the most logical way in which to spend one's energies would lie in perfecting one's ability to get the boat around the race course in the fastest way possible. That means practice, which can be pretty dull at times. It means blaming your inadequate performance on your own lack of ability, either temporary or chronic, rather than on your boat, the rating rule, your sails,

your crew, the weather and the 101 other things we all tend to blame.

"Don't misunderstand me. These things are all important. At the very top level of competition, where many of the contestants will sail virtually flawless races, they can be determinative. That level accounts for maybe one percent or less of all racing. In the other 99 percent, and as one works down, differences in skill play a larger and larger role in relation to differences in the technical aspects. In other words, the better sailor with mediocre equipment and an indifferent rating will beat the poorer sailer with perfect equipment and an optimized rating every time. It is a question of priorities. Sailing skill is paramount; everything else is subordinate" (*Yacht Racing,* June 1975).

The ensuing chapters are intended to do something about your sailing skill.

# [4]
# LAYING IT
# ON THE LINE

If you do not feel absolutely secure in your own mind about what it means to be ahead of another boat on a beat to windward, you should take time out to read and digest the opening paragraphs of Chapter 5 before continuing further.

Downwind starts are a thing of the past except in ocean racing. In this chapter we shall be looking at starting lines from which the first leg of the course is a beat to windward. The "favored end of the line" will always mean the end that is upwind of the other end. I shall try to avoid the terms "windward end" and "leeward end" commonly used to mean the committee end and the flag end. Dealing with these misnomers leads to recommendations like starting at the leeward end when it is to windward of the windward end, which may make sense to the cognoscenti but does add confusion to a scene that is already chaotic enough.

While on the subject of confusions, we ought to try to eliminate another one that could easily cost you a race. If I ask a crew member where a competitor is on a beat to windward and he answers, "Dead to leeward," I usually find that he means dead *abeam* on our leeward side, which is not the same thing at all. Dead to leeward means straight downwind from us. It could be expensive if you ask for the location of the windward mark and he says, "Dead to windward." If he means what he is saying, you sail on happily for a while. If he means that the mark bears abeam on the windward side, you had better get the hell about, fast; you are already overstanding. Make sure that you and your crew speak the same language.

One is reminded of what must be the world's best language-barrier sailing story, which Paul Elvstrom enjoys telling on himself.

A good line results in a good start.

Many years ago when he was Albert Debarge's crew in a Star Class World's Championship, Elvstrom spoke no French and Debarge no Danish, but both were quite proficient in English. Because he already had such a great reputation, Paul was expected to make some of the tactical decisions. After an excellent start Elvstrom, detecting a slight header, called "Tack!" Debarge, proudly showing off the fact that he knew at least one word of Danish, replied, "You're entirely welcome," and sailed serenely on.

But let's get back to starting a race.

The starting gun has just fired (smoke is rising from the stern of the committee boat); but the line is so bad that no one used the other end and there is a frightful jam at this end.

All the authorities stress the importance of a good start. If you are five yards behind at the start and in a bad position, you will in an astonishingly short time be fifty yards behind in a much worse position. So the books tell you to be at the preferred end of the line, with full headway, at gunfire. They then explain which is the preferred end—that's easy. What they don't specify is how to get there at the right time—and that's hard. It would not be hard except for one trifling difficulty: twenty skippers are trying to do exactly the same thing, and twenty boats cannot occupy the same space simultaneously.

There is a solution to the whole starting problem, but it depends not on you but on the race committee. I have been trumpeting this for half a lifetime and maybe it has done some good, maybe not. I'm perfectly willing to try once more. If the first mark is the windward mark, there is only one correct starting line: absolutely square to the wind. That means at right angles to the direction of the wind, with neither the flag end nor the committee end *the least bit* favored. A report from the race committee of the 1969 Star World's Championship states it well:

> "The smallest departure of the starting line from being absolutely square with the wind during the first two or three minutes of the preparatory period will certainly result in a bunching of contestants at the favored end. The line should be made square before the preparatory signal is made; this may be done successfully without a postponement if the adjustment is not too great. The adjustment of the starting line to accommodate a shift in the wind during the first three minutes or so of the preparatory period should be made under a postponement; otherwise there will not be time enough for contestants to sail to a better place along the line, and a poor start will result. (A Star could not sail the length of our starting line, which was a quarter mile long, in much less than four minutes.)"

I wish every race committee chairman could read that paragraph and take it to heart. It is obviously written by that rarity among committee men,

Too many boats for one starting line. If the helicopter is directly over any boats, it is making them very unhappy.

a good racing skipper. Note for instance that he wants to provide enough time for the skippers, not the committee, to get reorganized. Race committees, even good ones, sometimes get so wrapped up in the job that they begin to think of it as an end in itself and forget that they are out there only to help the contestants. The skippers, of course, should not forget that without race committees we would have no racing. Before you criticize them, remember that they are giving up their afternoon, many afternoons, for *you,* without a penny of recompense, solely because of their unselfish interest in the sport of yacht racing.

Stuart Walker on starting lines is even more positive (*The Tactics of Small Boat Racing,* W. W. Norton & Company, N.Y.): "No matter how good the race committee, no line is ever square to the wind. *One end is always favored* by virtue of being farther upwind" (italics his). He then goes on to explain what to do in case of doubt, which means that he has to admit that some lines are so good that it is hard to say which is the favored end. In that case he recommends starting at the flag or lefthand end to minimize backwind from boats on your lee bow. This means that in case of doubt the race committee should settle for a port end (the flag end of a marks-to-port line) that is dropped back ever so slightly from square. How many committees do this? They are far more likely to get a pretty good line set up and then *advance* the flag end, spoiling the whole thing.

If the line is square and long enough, the boats can spread out along the entire line without any feverish crowding of a favored end and the start is a relatively easy and peaceful operation. Alas, how seldom that happens! Let's face it, you have to learn how to deal with all the bad lines you are sure to encounter in a season's racing.

A general rule is to try to avoid the jam at the favored end. About a quarter to a fifth of the length of the line away from the good end is the closest you can go and be safe. If you can find or make for yourself a slot about there (Figure 3), you are golden. They are giving each other so

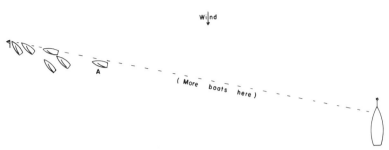

**Figure 3.** The flag is favored; boat *A* has a good position

much grief down there (or up there) in the mess, while you have reasonably clear air, that by the time you get settled down on the first leg you will find yourself not first, perhaps, but in a very respectable position, and without having risked fouling out or being recalled.

If the flag (lefthand end) is heavily favored, as unfortunately it often is, an alternative is the port-tack start. You run the line on the port tack, starting from the flag end shortly before gunfire, to leeward of everybody, searching for a hole in the wall of starboard-tack boats. With luck, one

All the starboard-tack boats are so tightly jammed together that they are bound to give one another a hard time. No. 4 may get the best start after all, even if she has to go astern of everyone.

FRANK GORDON

will develop soon—ideally, immediately astern of the first clump. If there is no hole there, bear off and keep looking. They are strapped down, interfering with each other, almost stalled out, and you are reaching with a full head of steam and can usually rush in where under ordinary conditions angels might fear to tread. It's risky, but not as bad as it sounds when you get accustomed to it. If worse comes to worst and you misjudge things, hold yourself and crew ready to slam her over onto starboard tack. You will then be in poor shape, second row center, so try to avoid that course except in an emergency. It's preferable to fouling out.

I find a typical entry in my log for August 5, 1972:

> "Incredibly bad line, which you could just cross on starboard with the aid of a favoring tide. Result, of course, a fierce jam at the pin with much crashing and a general recall. We made both first and second starts on port tack. A forest of masts came at us on starboard the second (and final) time; we had to go under almost all of them and still emerged about third because of our good headway. They were just stamping up and down, stopped almost dead, up there at the pin."

A port-tack start is virtually a must in a shifty northwester that has gone all the way over toward the west just at starting time. The port tack is now the lifted tack, and it is essential to get there without delay. Any distance sailed on starboard is being thrown away.

An extreme example of this occurred last summer. The committee set the starting line *and the course* during a period when a shifty northwester was indulging in a swing to the north. Then by our starting time it had gone back to west as far as it could go. Of course the lefthand (west) end was so favored that the line could barely be crossed on starboard tack. Marks happened to be left to starboard that day, so that the committee boat was stationed at the favored end (see Figure 4). You get the picture: a jam right under the noses of the committee, who could not fail to see that most of the fleet was over too soon. The result was two general recalls.

The port tack was so obviously desirable that about six boats tried it the first time. I think more would have done so had they realized that with the wind in this westerly phase you could actually lay the first mark on port. But the port-tack club kept losing members on each restart, so that on the third try only three of us were still game. The first two were a trifle too early and had to duck to leeward in search of a space. With about ten seconds to go, *Flame* found herself aiming for the favored spot at the lefthand end, with the first starboard tackers so far down, pinching and moving so slowly, that we had plenty of room to charge across, with a couple of seconds to spare, five feet from the committee boat. This was the impossible start, port tack at the favored end. We had not planned it that way but were more than happy to accept it when it fell into our laps. As

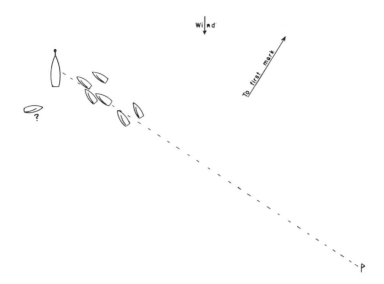

**Figure 4**

it turned out we did not lay the first mark, but only because we eased sheets too soon, and then were headed and had to take a short hitch. The same thing happened to everyone else, so we rounded first and that was it. There was no real windward work in the whole race and we just lengthened out all day to win the parade.

You may well ask why we were given so bad a line and such a poor course. The race was run by a club that holds one regatta per season. They

No. 5572 failed to fetch the pin end, visible just above the jibstay, and will jibe around as soon as the skipper can ease the mainsheet. Z5697 hit the mark, and is waiting to do the same.

arrived rather late with only the committee boat, no assisting launch, badly prepared and very shorthanded. They hurriedly set the line and course and started firing guns.

It is an interesting psychological fact that in a big regatta in which many classes have to be sent on their way at five-minute intervals the race committee becomes almost hypnotized by the sequence of signals and guns. There is a strong tendency to "let 'em go," get the first class started and then keep the show moving, even if something is obviously not quite as it should be. I have served on race committees often and have observed this phenomenon every time. Sometimes I am the lone voice crying for a correction, in which case my plea is usually disregarded. I well remember one occasion on which we, the committee, were trying to start thirty-five Lightnings on a line that was clearly much too short. There simply wasn't room to fit that many boats on the line, so, naturally, we had one general recall after another. I stated my opinion so positively that the chairman—a good friend before and since—has not invited me to serve again; but he never lengthened that line.

On the day of the race described above, the shorthanded committee should have taken time out to repair the damages after the first recall. But I can hear them saying, "Let them go on this course, it's good enough. The contestants don't want to wait any longer, they'd rather race." That's not true. They would *not* rather race. They would much prefer to wait, even if the committee boat, lacking a launch, had to up anchor to reset the line.

Race committees have my every sympathy. I understand their problems and know how many things can go wrong (usually simultaneously). I only wish to encourage them to keep trying. They dislike doing things that annoy the racing men. They should repeatedly be assured that a bad line or a bad course is a far worse annoyance than a postponement to make the necessary correction.

No one likes general recalls. They unfairly penalize the boats that actually made correct starts by letting off the violators scot-free. They encourage crowding and overaggressiveness at the next start, because you cannot afford to be left behind if this is going to be the one where the committee gives up and lets everyone go. The new one-minute rule helps but is not the final answer. There are those who believe that outright disqualification for being over the line too soon is the only ultimate cure. If you make a mistake out on the course you are not allowed a second chance; why not the same penalty for a premature start? This solution, being tried in some European racing areas, would greatly alter starting techniques and tactics. I rather doubt, however, whether the climate is right for such a change. The rule-making bodies seem to be tending in the opposite direction, toward making the penalties *less* severe. Already we have a rule allowing us to re-round a touched mark. If you make a premature start in the Bermuda Race you are not disqualified for failing to return, only some minutes (or hours) are added to your finish time. And fleets are even try-ing options for right-of-way violations, the 360, 720, and others.

The cure for general recalls is readily available: square the starting line and make it long enough, and the difficulty will usually evaporate. There are exceptions, but at least eight, probably nine, out of ten general recalls are caused by bad lines.

At present you are stuck with the general recall and must live with it, so you might as well make the best possible use of it. After a general recall nearly all of the skippers will try exactly the same start over again. You should plan accordingly. If the committee makes no attempt to improve the line, the same jam will occur at the same place. If you were in it before, stay out of it this time. If you liked your first start you now have a chance to polish it up and make it an even better one.

Whenever a new crew member comes aboard, there are so many things you have to tell him to do that you usually forget to tell him what not to do. If a new man is doing the timing you must remember to tell him *not* to stop the stopwatch when the starting gun goes off. If this is in fact not the starting gun but a general recall, you start again five minutes later and he has lost his timing with no way to recover it. The same thing ap-

Good skippers make precision starts, even in big boats. No. 7982 carries a "slab reef" in the main.

plies at a postponement. The timekeeper starts his watch on the first gun, and when it is followed by a second gun there is apparently a strong reflex impulse to stop the watch. Some sort of subconscious mental process says, "The start is being held up so I should hold up the timing too." There are strong and loud instructions on the *Flame:* "Once the watch is started, *always* leave it running." Tell them it is good for the watch to let it run down —anything, to get them in the habit of leaving it running. All this of course presupposes that you have the right kind of stopwatch. A watch with a hand that sweeps across a single arc down to zero, without repeating, might as well be thrown overboard. You *must* have a repeater, one that reads down the last five minutes and then goes around again, and again.

We always start at least two watches, sometimes three, on the ten-minute gun. Then I take off mine, an ordinary wrist chronograph with sweep hand, and stow it away for an emergency. To date our Swiss racing timer has never let us down, but the day it quits (fifty seconds before the start) I don't want to be left gasping.

It is a rare start that decides the whole race. Usually all you need is reasonably clear air and some headway, and you will soon be absorbed in problems and tactical situations that have more bearing on the final outcome than the start. The light fluky day is typically one on which the start hardly matters. The fleet is juggled so many times on its way around the course that there are plenty of chances for recovery after a poor start. Sometimes there is even an advantage in *not* starting well on such a day. The boats that start last and split with the fleet, taking in desperation what may seem to be the wrong tack, as often as not wind up in the lead at the first mark. Not so on a steady day. You must weigh the risk of a good start against the recovery potential for that day. Howard McMichael, Sr., never makes spectacular starts, preferring to hold back and stay out of harm's way. He is one of the best light-air artists in the game, once collecting a string of five consecutive firsts in our class, an unheard-of performance, all in light and fluky races and all with conservative starts.

When the starboard end of the line is the favored end, you must expect a great jam to develop up there. If that end is only slightly favored I much prefer starting somewhere down the line. It is a great relief to have plenty of space. You can time your start perfectly and cross under full headway without a care in the world. You then look up to windward and there they all are, bearing only slightly aft of abeam and looking as if they are way ahead—but not for long. You have clear air while most of them are bothering each other, and in a very short space of time you are out in the number 2 or 3 slot, a bargain at the very low price of no risk at all. If the starboard end was favored because it was the northerly side on a shifty northwest day, you will be even better off when the expected westerly header arrives.

If there is a following current (tide) or a current carrying you down the line from right to left, the best start at a crowded starboard end is the

Second row, center, is no place to be with a wall of boats up ahead.

slightly delayed approach. Come in closehauled on starboard tack, aiming a little above the committee boat and a little late, and let them all cross your bow on their way to the line. They will get there too soon and will have no choice but to ride down the line while you luff across their sterns for the desired weather berth.

If there is no current and a good breeze there is just one perfect start on a starboard favored line, attained by the boat that has things timed to arrive at the right spot with full rights and full headway. It's not easy to do, but it's sometimes fun trying because the risk is small. If you are too early you will have to go around the committee boat to re-start, but at least you'll still be at the correct end. Once last summer we found ourselves hard on the wind on starboard tack headed for the stern of the committee boat with a minute to go. There were boats hanging around up to windward hoping to barge, and I was naïvely expecting them to go away. No one says anything on the *Flame* during the final minute before gunfire except the timekeeper, whose steady monotone is giving me the countdown. But with about forty seconds left the jib-sheet tender could stand it no longer and jolted me into reality and action by saying urgently, "Call them up!" So we spent the next half minute shouting for our rights, and one by one the others luffed or went about or faded away until, with about ten seconds remaining, only one was left sitting dead in the water square across our path on a reaching course, her skipper looking scared to death, which was not surprising with the bow of our boat aimed at full speed for the middle of his cockpit. Everything had gone so well up to now that I was damned if I wanted to spoil it all by bearing away, which would have cost us our timing and our weather berth. So I took the much riskier alternative of luffing around the other boat's stern by jamming the tiller down as far as it would go. We missed her transom and were able to bear off again without hitting the committee boat, I don't know how, to make what my crew called *the* start of the summer. They enjoyed it much more than I did.

No matter how badly a boat fouls you, especially at the start, try to avoid running into her. First of all if you collide you may both be disqualified under Rule 32 or Rule 67, 1. More important is the necessity of avoiding damage to the boat, not to mention your position in the race. Even a slight collision may result in a serious loss of time getting clear. It is preferable to avoid the jam no matter what rights you have, get out of there, and get started in the race. My notes on another occasion say:

> "Until five minutes before the start the line was very good. Then the wind shifted about 30° to the north, allowing us actually to lay the first mark on starboard and of course creating a fearful jam at the committee end. M—, K—, and I think G— were early, all over the place in the way on port tack etc., and *we all sort of steered around them* [emphasis added]. We had an excellent start, probably no more than 3 or 4 seconds late in a relatively clear space about three boats down from the committee. Nos. 24 and 25, above us, soon faded because the wind gradually headed."

Under favorable conditions a "dip start" occasionally works. The conditions are a strong current with the wind and rather light air, so that the fleet is having a hard time staying on the line. It is now easy to come down from the wrong side of the line, dropping into any space that you can find. In extreme conditions it is not even necessary to find a space, because the boats that think they are on the line are being swept to leeward in a sagging arc. You simply sail along the real line to weather of them all and at gunfire you are home free. Don't try a dip start without an adverse

The "hover start" is not practical under today's rules.

HAL WILLIAMS

The fleet hits the line with full headway at the start of a Bermuda Race.

current. And *don't* try it after a general recall; if you do you are automatically disqualified under the one-minute rule (51.1 (c)).

Some authorities have recommended the "hovering" start, in which you park on the line barely holding steerageway until just before gunfire. This used to work in small centerboard boats, but it doesn't work in any boats under current rules. You have no rights, and almost immediately someone will obtain an overlap to leeward and start shouting, "Get ready to come up; *up! UP!*" and there you are, having been luffed over, looking for a nonexistent hole to return and re-start.

Starting tactics differ widely between dinghies and large keel boats. In ocean racers the timing is all-important. You start on a formula (reach off, go about, reach back) and hope that not too many others are using your formula in your immediate vicinity. If things go wrong there is not much to be done about it. I was once privileged to sail an American Yacht Club cruise aboard the late Commodore de Coursey Fales's schooner *Nina*. Being navigator, I had to judge the timing of the final approach. Everything would have been dandy except that the wind freshened at the critical moment and we came flying down to the port end of the starting line, which happened to be the committee end, with sheets slightly eased, going faster and faster with the time running out too slowly. When we had about twenty seconds left I said, "Can you slow her a little?" The Commodore gave me a pitying glance and held off as long as he could, but you do not slow a sixty-foot schooner under full sail in a fresh breeze. The gentlemen on the committee boat had a spectacular if scary view of a bowsprit aiming straight at them until at the last moment we swung up to cross the line three seconds too soon. The Commodore, completely unruffled, jibed around the committee boat, and we re-crossed on port behind most of the fleet. This ultimately resulted in our sailing into Smithtown Bay, not normally a good course down the Sound but this time, for once, a winner, redeeming my mistake by sheer good luck.

I sailed most of one Block Island Week on a 46-foot cutter. Again I had signed on as navigator, and was dumfounded when the owner remarked casually, twenty minutes before the first start, "You have made more starts than any of us, take the helm for this one." I thought he was joking and tried my best to refuse, but he insisted, and he was the boss. I was the starting helmsman for three days and it worked out better than he had any right to expect. We had one fair start, one poor one, and the final one was a beauty. We won the race week in our division, but for other reasons. I think putting a total stranger to the boat at the helm for the start without time to get acquainted even with her turning radius was a dangerous risk. I found out the hard way that they did something else on that boat of which I do not approve. Until I shut them up in no uncertain language, various members of the crew were trying to contribute critical advice right up to the starting gun. I am convinced that only one man can start the boat: too much is happening too fast to weigh extraneous opinions at the last second. The helmsman must stand or fall on his own instant decisions. No boat can be started by committee.

Many sailors, including all those of less than middle age, do not realize how easy life has been made for us by modern practice. Until about the time of World War II, most race instructions consisted of a preassigned course. A "reverse course" signal at race time meant go around the other way; but no other change was possible. More races started downwind than upwind, with consequent unbelievable jams at the first mark. How to avoid or extract yourself from the chaos at the first leeward mark became a more important consideration than a good start. So much sheer luck was involved that yachtsmen clamored for and eventually obtained the now almost universally used windward start. Downwind starts still occur, but only in ocean races, where the fleet becomes unscrambled long before it reaches the first mark.

# [5]
# THE WINDWARD LEG: TECHNIQUES

On a windward leg, what boat is in the lead? *Not* necessarily the boat nearest the mark in straight-line distance, but the boat that is farthest to windward. You are ahead of another boat if you are on the windward side of a line drawn through the other boat and at right angles to the wind direction; otherwise you are behind that boat. This is on condition that neither of you can fetch the windward mark without some more tacking.

In Figure 5, the committee end $(B_1)$ of the starting line is nearer the first mark than the flag end $(A_1)$. But if the wind is steady, no distance is gained by starting at $B_1$. The two boats will be even when they get to the line marked $A_2B_2$. They were always even, because they were always equally far from the mark in distance measured directly to leeward from the mark. Nevertheless, on a first leg of this kind there will usually be a jam at the committee end of the line, because everyone is anxious to get on the port tack as soon as possible. If the flag end is favored slightly, here is an excellent opportunity to gain a few lengths at no extra charge: start where there is lots of room at the less popular port end, tack as soon as you can, and you'll be that much ahead of the committee-end crowd.

*Why* must you get onto the port tack on this leg? Because it is the tack that aims the boat more nearly in the direction of the mark. If the wind is absolutely steady the starboard tack is just as good—for a while. But how many winds are steady? In a shifty breeze, the starboard tack is very risky, as we shall presently see.

Every boat has an optimum sailing angle on the wind; trying to point higher will only slow the boat down. For the sake of simplicity this angle is frequently assumed to be 45°, meaning that

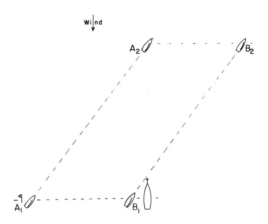

**Figure 5**

the boat tacks through 90°. Modern well-designed keel boats do much better than that, especially in a good breeze. If you think you need 90° in such a boat you will badly overstand every mark. Draw a pencil line on the weather deck, not at right angles to the keel but angled slightly forward. Sight along this line when closehauled, then go about and see whether you fetch above or below the point sighted. When you are satisfied that you have determined just how high the boat points under average to good sailing conditions, draw or paint permanent tacking lines on the deck (Figure 6). On the *Flame* our lines aim 18° forward of abeam; in other words, we tack through 72°. Under optimum conditions of smooth water and a brisk offshore breeze we do a little better than that, and have to tack for the mark before it bears 18° forward of abeam.

There is a diamond of available water that you can use without penalizing yourself on every windward leg. If your boat tacks through 90°, your diamond is a square; a higher-pointing boat has a correspondingly narrower diamond (Figure 7). The top two sides of the diamond are the lay lines.

**Figure 6.** 18 ° lines, for tacking through 72 °

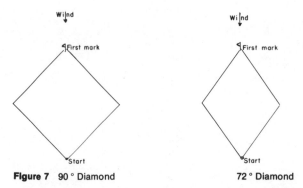

**Figure 7**  90 ° Diamond              72 ° Diamond

Every foot sailed outside the diamond (beyond the lay lines) is wasted, and you should be on the other tack, heading for the mark.

On a course like that of Figure 5 the diamond is very lopsided (Figure 8). The necessity of staying inside it is one reason for getting on the port tack immediately; but there is a much more important reason having to do with headers.

A header on one tack is a lift on the opposite tack; hence of course the rule, "Tack on headers." In Figure 9, the two boats are even with each other ($A_1B_1$) before the shift. But $A_4$ crosses $B_4$ easily by tacking on the header, because as soon as the header arrives, $A$ is automatically ahead of $B$ relative to the new cross-wind line. There is no way $B$ can gain on this shift; but she can hope to stay even with $A$ by tacking also at the windshift line. Instead of holding port tack she should tack at position $B_3$. Then if the wind ever goes back to where it was, they will be level again.

All the above is elementary and in all the books. An understanding of why it is so important to tack on headers is essential to the successful planning of the windward leg. Now it should be clear why the starboard tack is so unsafe in Figure 5. If the wind shifts to the right, the boats on that side can tack and cross the others because there is not enough room in the narrow diamond for them to tack too and wait for a return shift. If the

**Figure 8.**  Lopsided 72 ° diamond

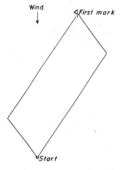

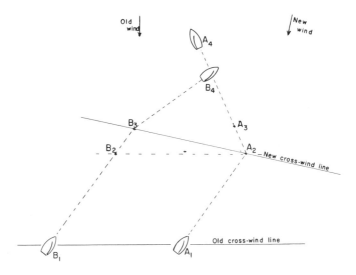

**Figure 9**

wind shifts to the left, the starboard tack gains, to be sure; but it must shift left only so much, and not enough to allow the whole fleet to lay the mark or nearly lay the mark. Thus the margin of safety for the skipper starting and staying on starboard tack is extremely small and getting smaller as he approaches the lefthand lay line.

The narrow diamond (lopsided windward leg) is particularly likely to develop in a northwester. Everything combines to make the situation potentially hazardous. The shifty breeze makes it almost impossible for the race committee to set a windward mark that will stay to windward; the breeze is offshore (on the East Coast) and brisk, making for very high pointing; and the boats are traveling fast through smooth water. Under these conditions there is definite danger of overstanding on *both* tacks. If the course starts out lopsided, get on the tack taking you toward the mark early and at all costs and *stay* on that tack, even if it means ducking under every boat you meet on starboard. To allow yourself to be trapped into tacking under the lee bow of some clown who is hypnotized by the power of the starboard tack is a fatal error under these conditions. By the time you get back onto port, half the fleet may be around the mark.

It has always been assumed that, if you have overstood the mark whether by bad luck or bad planning, you can generally recoup some of your loss by easing sheets and reaching in at a slightly higher speed. Harold Vanderbilt, in *On the Wind's Highway,* wrote: "When we tacked for the mark, the Challenger looked like a rather badly beaten boat. She stood on for a couple of minutes before tacking and subsequently drove for the mark with a hard full and perhaps with eased sheets. Now, for the first time, she showed her speed and overhauled us at an astonishing rate, so that our lead was reduced to 18 seconds by the time we rounded the mark." This is an extreme example pointing up the fact that a J-boat could reach much faster than it could go to windward. The same happens to be true for a Star. Height of mast compared to length of boom is called the aspect-ratio of the mainsail. For both a J-boat and a Star boat, this aspect-ratio is 2:1; the hoist is about twice the length of the boom. But on an E-22 the aspect-ratio is nearly 3:1. As a partial result, the boat is very fast closehauled, and does *not* pick up any appreciable speed as sheets are eased. This can make a marked difference in racing strategy. For one thing, it greatly increases the importance of staying inside the lay lines of the diamond.

Another effect of a high aspect-ratio is to reduce the distance within which a safe leeward position is effective. If two E-22's are a boat length apart with the leeward one slightly ahead but not clear ahead (the two boats are overlapped), they can sail side by side in this position without apparently affecting each other, whereas with two boats of lower aspect-ratio the leeward boat would very quickly pull ahead while at the same time pointing higher. This means that you can sail over a boat that has tacked under your lee bow more easily in a high- than in a low-aspect-ratio boat. Conversely, if you on the port tack are converging with a starboard tack boat on collision course, think twice before trying to tack in lee. It is better to bear off and go astern if he is going to sail over you anyway.

The science of yacht design is developing so rapidly that an aspect-ratio of 3:1, at least for boats with masthead genoas, is already out of date. Many of the current (1976) fast ocean racers carry a mainsail aspect-ratio of 4:1; but these boats have such a huge genoa that the whole aerodynamic system is different, and I am not talking about this type of sail plan.

Perhaps you expected to find some hints on tuning under this chapter heading. Sorry, but I can't tune your boat from this distance. The whole rig must be assembled as a unit, and everything is interdependent, including how you sail. I am not a great tuning addict. If things are right, the boat will go. If she doesn't go, don't sit there in a gloomy rage; do something about it. But by "something" I do not mean fiddling with turnbuckles.

No. 5596 could not quite get clear, as shown by the second picture.

DUNDLER ALBERT

Too much weather helm. Getting the jib up all the way and moving the sheets around a bit would probably help. But Skipper, what are you doing in a jacket and tie?

That sort of change must be made before the race. What to do during the race is trim, not tune. Try the sheets an inch farther out or in, or move the jib leads or the main traveler, or the outhaul, or the backstay. On a day when things are going badly and you are losing anyway, you might as well experiment, especially if the breeze is steady and you have another boat near by to compare with. The correct trim for your boat, sailed by you, with your sails, is a matter of trial and error for each type of wind and sea, and no one else can tell you what to do.

Modern racing boats are so fast that everything we do slows them down. Try to figure out what you are doing that is holding the boat back. Other boats are going fast; yours should be able to do the same if you would only let her. Relax a little, loosen your death-grip on the tiller, and give her her head.

It is a remarkable but often observed phenomenon that many skippers need a guide boat for optimum performance. They sail best alongside someone else, and can keep up with you for half the windward leg if they are near enough; but the minute they go off by themselves you never see them again. This means that they have been trimming and steering the boat by your example. When you separate, their attention wanders, they start thinking about the wrong things, and inevitably the boat is sailed poorly. I know

AL AUDLEMAN, GULF YACHTING

A firm grip on the mainsheet, a light touch on the tiller, and a keen eye on the sail.

of no occupation that requires more uninterrupted concentration than an afternoon's race in a small boat.

The ability to sail well to windward without being in company with other boats is indispensable in a fog. Foggy weather is rare in most localities, but occasionally it provides a real test of keeping the boat up to speed, solo, and it also turns the race into something that seldom occurs in small boats, a navigator's race. From my log of September 6, 1971:

> "After a calm sunny morning with southwest zephyrs it turned to east at 11:15, and by 11:45 was blowing pretty briskly, with fog. We waited at the mooring until we had less than an hour to starting time, and even then we arrived too soon in a 15-to-20 knot easterly. Where it all came from I couldn't fathom. Southwest was the forecast.
>
> "We started off to $W$ [a mid-Sound marker] with the wind at $90°$ I think. It was hard to get things accurate in the wind and spray. It seemed more sanitary to go in toward Hempstead, so we did after a mediocre start and not apparently going very well as we had to go under three boats' sterns in order to get away on port. Chugged off to windward comfortably enough, with the jib very flat and the main traveler eased maybe 10 inches. That soon seemed far too much, and we kept drawing it in until it was back to normal moderate weather trim, about 4 inches off the center line. Nobody around in the fog except No. 47, who unaccountably stayed with us, which made me think we had the slows.

US 658 will soon move into the lead from this position.

"We were keeping track of the time, so after a while we tacked (on the watch) in order to go past *L* [an intermediate mark] and take a new departure from there. All worked as planned, except that we were always arriving early. We seemed to be making 5½ knots through the water on the wind, much more than it felt like. Eventually along came Skip Etchells out of the fog, on the other tack, well astern. Surprise. Finally more surprises as we neared *W:* they all showed up astern. We must have had good boatspeed, because we gradually pulled out on Skip; but also it may have shifted 5 or 10 degrees toward the south, because we were heading 60° on starboard near the mark, which calls for about a 97° wind direction."

Here is Evan Dailey's description of the last race of the 1973 Star Class World's Championship, sailed in the Pacific off San Diego. Many boats got lost in the fog that day, including the five leaders; 31 of 55 starters failed to finish.

"After about two and a half hours of postponing to wait for the fog to lift, the race finally started. There was reasonably good wind, about 8 knots, but still so foggy that it was difficult to see the other end of the line from the committee boat. The first leg seemed to favor the right side of the course. We rounded sixth, with Eckart Wagner in the lead for the whole first round. During the reaching legs the fog lifted, and the second round (windward leeward) was sailed under blue skies in a nice breeze. As we rounded the last leeward mark, still in sixth place, the fog started to roll in again, and in fifteen minutes the leading boats were completely out of sight. The next boats behind us were just barely visible. We favored the right side again, as the wind was constantly shifting toward a more northerly direction. My crew, Mike Cooper, kept time on his stopwatch as to how long we were on each tack. We finally spotted an amber light just to weather of our course. We sailed on this port tack for about five minutes, carefully watching the light move to the left. When we came about we could make out the committee boat with its cluster of spectator boats. When we crossed the line there were a lot of guns fired and other noise. Mike said he thought we had won. We sailed over to the committee boat to find out, and sure enough we had."

The Stars encountered a different problem in their World's Championship the following year, caused by the difficulty of finding marks in a rough sea. This event was sailed in the Atlantic Ocean off Laredo, Spain, where conditions are really rugged in a northerly. In the fifth race, after rounding the windward mark the first group squared away on what they thought was the course to the next mark. They all headed much too high. Navigation is by no means easy in a 22-foot boat when everything is jumping all over the place including the compass. Perhaps the leader led them astray and all the rest followed. They were having so much fun on a roaring exhilarat-

They look about even; but anything can happen so close to the shore, where the wind is surely very shifty.

HAL WILLIAMS

ing plane most of the time that they gave too little thought to where they were heading, until suddenly—no reaching mark. There was supposed to be a yacht flying a balloon accompanying each mark. But you cannot anchor a gas-filled balloon with an iron chain, nor even with a strong rope; and today all the balloons simply blew away. Other extenuating circumstances (as usual) added to the confusion. The mark was very hard to see against a dark rocky shore under lowering clouds. Furthermore, two days previously, in exactly similar circumstances, the whole crowd had all gone too far to *leeward* of the course; so this time they overcompensated. The upshot was that some of the more careful navigators found the mark exactly where it was supposed to be, to round far ahead of the erstwhile leaders. The first three places in that race went to series outsiders.

The sixth and last race produced a different and theoretically simpler problem. By now the three series leaders had their places safely tucked away and elected to sit this one out. We have the account of the sixth-race winner, Arnold Osterwalder of Switzerland.

> "Max Juchli, a newcomer from the Bodensee Fleet in Switzerland, arrived at the first mark 100 yards ahead of Osterwalder, Hamberg and Steinmayer. The leeward marks could again this day be seen only from rather short distance, but could be found with compass, course 315 and 225 respectively. The committee boat showed and hailed a new windward compass bearing of 20° for the second beat. The wind had freshened already during the reaches to 6–10 knots. On starboard tack one could fetch 10°, which induced me to follow this tack whereas Juchli did not cover and sailed well away to the right on the port tack, thus overstanding the mark. We were attacked to windward by Hamberg and Kim Fletcher, who in the meantime had also come up. Our defense by means of a tack was too late and the now leading boats tacked as well. To avoid overstanding we tacked back. Hamberg and Fletcher, who easily could have covered us, showed no inclination to do so and let us go. They obviously thought the old reaching mark was the new windward mark. We therefore arrived at the windward mark considerably ahead of everybody else. Way back followed Larry Whipple and Josi Steinmayer, who had passed the overstanding boats. On the run we actually lapped the last competitor, reaching the finish 4½ minutes ahead of the second boat," an enormous lead in a world's championship race.

Evan Dailey concluded his account of the last race of the 1973 Star series quoted earlier by modestly remarking that the race might have been "a little unfair to the five boats that probably should have finished ahead of us." I disagree. The modern trend is too much toward lead boats, foolproof windward legs, and colored smoke bombs. All we lack is a magnet pulling the boats toward the weather mark. If the smallest thing happens out of the ordinary, up goes the cry, "Cancel the race!" It seems to me that the ability to rise to the occasion and cope with an emergency is a perfectly valid part of sailing a race, and that those unable to do so need not be granted an automatic second chance.

While on the subject of special techniques we ought to mention the much argued topic of lee-bowing the tide. (The tide goes up and down; what moves horizontally is current. Therefore to be accurate one should speak of lee-bowing the current, but the other usage has become customary.)

If you are sailing on a windward leg so that one tack heads the boat exactly against the current—that is, you have the current right on the nose —you may be in a position to gain by lee-bowing it. If you can succeed in pinching so that you can point the slightest amount higher without noticeably decreasing your speed, your boat will be carried to windward (sideways) by the lee-bow current, as compared with a boat that remains headed into the current or, worse, falls off slightly below the direction from which the current is moving.

You may encounter the right conditions for an effective lee-bow very seldom, perhaps once a season, perhaps even less frequently. But when it does occur, the process is so spectacular that you will never forget it. All the salt-water experts have noted it from time to time and been duly impressed. They do not question that it happens; they only wonder why it happens. Yet some people theorize that there can be no such phenomenon. These skeptics argue as follows: If two boats are sailing in the same body of water it should be immaterial to them whether the whole body of water is stationary or moving, in whatever direction. If a one-knot current is running from west to east, and you are racing toward some mark to the west, you would have exactly the same race if you stopped the current and let the mark be towed toward the west at one knot. Now where is your lee-bow effect? Or, they say, it's just like two airplanes maneuvering in the sky. Their positions relative to each other do not change whether there is a west wind or an east wind or no wind.

Both these analogies are false, and for the same reason. Both would be valid for power boats (or even better, submarines), which take their motive force from the medium through which they are moving, like airplanes, and track their courses over a second medium, the bottom. But a sailboat moves through the water, over the bottom, and takes its power from a *third* medium, the air, which is also moving, and in a direction different from that of the water. A kite would be a better (though imperfect) analogy. The moving air streams past the kite as the current streams past the boat, and the kite string plays the role of the force of the sails that are driving the boat. If two kites were flying steadily side by side, the slightest amount of "rudder" on one of them would cause it to yaw rapidly away

SUE CUMMINGS

It would be unwise to pass so close to the windward mark if it were anything more than a rubber ball. If it has a stick with a flag on it, give it a wider berth than you think necessary.

from the other one. A boat moored in a tideway does the same thing. These are illustrations of a magnified lee-bow effect.

I ought to be able to draw a diagram with vector arrows explaining

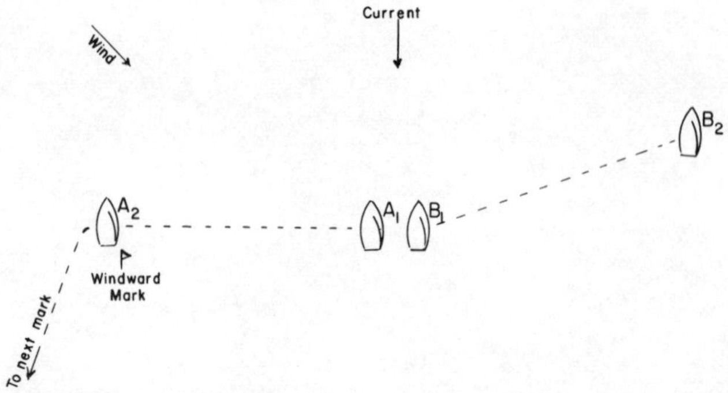

**Figure 10**

the whole phenomenon. Unfortunately I'm not a good enough physicist, and if I were I expect that the resulting diagram would be too complicated to be of much help. To illustrate what goes on, an extreme example would be that of Figure 10. A strong current is holding the boats stationary or almost stationary. Although they are moving through the water in a light breeze, they are making no progress over the bottom. From position $A_1$, boat $A$, by very slight pinching to windward, gets the current under her lee bow, is shoved sideways to position $A_2$, and takes off for the next mark. Boat $B$ either stays at $B_1$ wondering what happened, or, by bearing off slightly, is pushed sideways to $B_2$, in which case I give her some forward motion because she is full and by instead of pinching. But note that that forward motion is no bargain. Not only is she going away from the mark, but she is still well to leeward of it. None of these things would happen without any current. New forces are created by the motion of the supporting medium (the water) over the reference frame (the bottom) that simply disappear when that motion disappears.

I have heard the following attempted explanation of the lee-bow effect, to which I cannot subscribe. When a boat is sailing to windward the apparent wind is drawn forward of the direction of the true wind. The helmsman then sails the boat as high as she will profitably go relative to this apparent wind. If an adverse current slows the boat to a dead stop, as in the example of Figure 10, then the apparent wind returns to the direction of the true wind; the apparent wind is fairer than it was before, by virtue of which the boat can be pointed higher and thus acquire the desired lee-bow effect.

Two flaws are apparent here. The first is that both boats would be doing the same thing, creating no differential. Without a slight difference in sailing angle you can't make the lee-bow work to your advantage over another boat. The other flaw is subtler and depends on something more fundamental. If indeed a fairing of the apparent wind means that you can point higher, why can't you point higher than the norm immediately after going about? I'm talking now about an ordinary tack in light air with no tide involved. The boat is moving slowly, having lost way, on the new tack, and the apparent wind must therefore be farther aft than it will be when you have gathered full headway. Can you point *higher* immediately after tacking? On the contrary, many skippers find it necessary to bear off for a few seconds. (I believe that that is wrong too, but let us not confuse the present issue.) Yes, the apparent wind is fairer when you are stopped; *but it is also weaker*. Sometimes a sizable percentage of the velocity of the apparent wind is created by the boat's forward motion against the wind. The boat wants to point higher in stronger, not weaker, breezes. It appears that in light to moderate airs the two effects about counterbalance each other: the favorable direction of the apparent wind immediately after tacking is offset by its decreased velocity.

I suggested that a normal full-and-by course should be assumed immediately after any well executed tack. Do not pinch, but do not fill away too far either, and especially do not change the trim. In order to help the jib-sheet tender maintain identical trim on both tacks your jib sheets should be permanently marked (we sew in colored threads), so that he can go to the same mark without asking. The only exception is in extremely light air, when it may be necessary to reach off in order to gain headway enough to regenerate the apparent wind. The best rule in such conditions is, don't tack at all, or at least keep the tacking down to an absolute minimum.

I once had the good fortune to be a guest observer at a southern winter sailing school. The participants were racing skippers and their families who were there to sharpen up their techniques. The boats were Solings. It was heartening and indeed amazing to see the improvement achieved in a single week of concentrated racing practice and instruction under the expert guidance of the school's staff. Of course many faults had to be corrected. Most skippers bore off too far after tacking in a good breeze. More interesting was another habit some had formed: they bore off noticeably just *before* tacking, as if they thought that it was necessary somehow to gather speed to carry the boat through the tack. This bearing away is a real loser. Not only does it carry the boat unnecessarily to leeward, but also it results in the necessity of turning the hull through a larger angle to complete the tack. Any turning is a slowing operation. The best skippers tend to do just the opposite; they start their tack by momentarily pinching slightly in order to reduce the amount of the final turn. In rough water it is also important to choose a relatively smoother interval in which to make the tack.

Class J yachts used to go so fast in light air that they "made their own wind" to an astonishing degree. Vanderbilt described bringing the apparent wind forward 90° on a reach (in *On the Wind's Highway*).

"Gradually, almost imperceptibly, we picked up speed. Foot by foot we slowly trimmed the sheets and bore off gradually to our course. It was at least four minutes after rounding before *Ranger* gathered full way, about 10 knots under these conditions. The apparent wind, judging from the fly at the masthead, was about 4 points on the bow. All sheets were trimmed almost flat aft, they had just enough lift to give her plenty of life. We took our ballooner off the stay as soon as it became apparent that we could not use it. The actual wind was about 4 points on the quarter, and the angle between it and the apparent wind was about 90°. It requires very unusual and special conditions to draw the wind ahead to this extent."

The velocity vectors do not work out quite right (they seldom do.) At 10 knots, with a 10-knot real breeze 4 points off the quarter, the resultant wind should appear 6 points off the bow, not 4. So the true wind must have been even less than the boat's speed. That is not impossible. Iceboats go faster than the wind most of the time, and catamarans often do.

# [6]
# THE WINDWARD LEG: STRATEGY

Before the start but after you have had time to assimilate all the available weather signs and decide more or less what kind of day it is going to be, you should plan a general strategy for the day's race. This race plan takes into consideration factors depending on the series involved, your standing and that of nearby competitors, the opportunities offered by the course that has been signaled, your boat's probable performance level in today's weather conditions, and most important of all, what is the wind going to do next.

Many modern courses start with a windward leg, followed by some downwind work and then some kind of second round. In our E-22 fleet the underlying series, on which some others are superimposed, is an all-summer affair of thirty-odd races for the championship of the Yacht Racing Association of Long Island Sound. Our main objective is to do well in the YRA series, which is also our fleet championship and the eliminations for the Nationals. On board the *Flame* I am afraid we give too much thought to our present and future standing in the championship, at the expense of today's race. This is wrong. The best way to build up a good season's score is to win today's race. In theory the season's standings should be disregarded, at least for the first half of the summer. In practice this is easier said than done.

One of the top members of our fleet, Robert (Bubbles) Shattuck, has developed what seems to me to be a highly intelligent race strategy. On the first windward leg he disregards the competition altogether and sails the leg the way he has previously decided ought to be best for the day. If that works he arrives at the windward mark in the lead and devotes the rest of the race to covering this position. If it fails he has the rest of the race in which to bail himself out. By following this prescription he won the 1974 season.

The success of this race (and series) plan depends heavily on the ability of the skipper to sail a good first leg. The 1974 winner did not have outstanding boat speed to windward; in fact on steady days he had a hard time keeping up with the best. Therefore his high average speaks eloquently for his ability to go the right way at the right time.

A few words about this matter of boat speed. If you can make your boat go noticeably faster than anyone else's to windward, your worries are over and you will win the series anyway, almost regardless of strategy. But that can happen only until the rest of the fleet catches on. They then adopt whatever it is that is making you go, and you are back with the pack again. It is an interesting phenomenon that these temporary bursts of speed occur only in the smaller (usually centerboard) classes. The reason is that permissible changes have a greater effect on small boats. Moving the mast two inches may make a new boat out of a 15-footer, whereas the same change in a 30-footer might go unnoticed. Even if you moved the 30-footer's mast four inches the proportional change would not make for the same speed change.

There are dozens of gadgets on a boat of one of the small "hot" classes, all of which are in constant interplay and all of which affect trim and speed. The position, agility, and reaction time of the crew, certainly the touch of the helmsman, are more important on a small boat than on a large one. Dennis Surtees, describing his performance in the last race of the 1974 World's Championship of the 5-0-5 Class, writes:

> "I hadn't allowed for current and finished up [the maneuver] wrapped around the mark. With the fleet as bunched as it had been, I finally came out of this about 35th. . . . We thought we were out altogether. We were, but not too badly. We finished sixth in the end, by virtue of what seemed to be quite superior speed upwind. On each tack we seemed to be lifted above our neighbors when we held the same speed, and when we let her foot our boat simply jumped forward" (*Yacht Racing,* November 1974).

This could never happen in a larger keel boat, especially while struggling through the backwind of thirty boats in a world's championship. In a keelboat fleet, a short lead at the first mark is all you can hope for, but it may be enough for the day. That is why the first-leg strategy is so important.

Specifically, what am I talking about? What are you supposed to *do* to win the first leg? Mainly, the answer is, Go the right way. Take the right tack at the start, and have the courage to stay on that tack if it looks temporarily poor but is eventually going to pay off. Watch the rest of the fleet, but only for guidance. When they peel off one by one and try the other direction, as they always do, detail one of your crew to watch carefully how they are making out over there. Sometimes you can judge by their performance relative to each other. If the other tack loses out each time, you know you are golden; if the other tack wins each time, your strategy for the day may be the wrong one. But don't give up your master plan without a struggle, and don't give it up too soon. Hear Olympic gold medalist David Forbes:

> "If the wind is lifting on the weather [starboard] side you've got to be prepared to tack early and go behind some boats to get to the lifting side. So to me the twenty minutes or half hour before the start are extremely important to establish what's going to happen, because at the time of the gun if you don't know where you should be going you can forget the race. . . . I love to start with a knocking wind, and if I'm on the knocking leg after the start I'll stick on that knock until everybody else is gone. And if I can stay on the weather side of the next lift I'm happy as a lark, but if I'm snowed in and I'm a leeward boat and the wind is lifting I'll dive off and go behind four or five boats if necessary to get to the lifting side. . . .
>
> "When I started sailing overseas I used to get behind and then try to do the impossible and look for magic boat speed that just isn't there. The whole object is not to get behind in the first place and you can best do this by starting well and sailing well on your first beat. But if you get behind I think the best thing you can do is forget the guys around you and sail your boat as fast as you can, using the techniques which you know are good, thinking about your course, tacking in the shifts and taking no notice of the rest of the fleet."

The decision to swallow your losses, abandon your plan, and go scurrying over to the other side as fast as possible in pursuit of the leaders is always a difficult one. It depends on instant analysis of the day's probable weather vagaries. In a standard northwester that shifts back and forth with a semi-regular phase, you may get a strong lift, look up over your shoulder, and find them all abeam to weather. If that happens, *don't panic:* this is not the time to tack. Wait, sail on, and the wind will return, eventually heading you so much that you can then tack and cross them all. This is the essence of sailing a northwester, and it can be a lot of fun.

If, on the other hand, you have reason to think that the shift that has put them ahead is a permanent one, then you must get into that shift even if it means starting the race over again from a disadvantaged position. To stay in your initial bad place will only make matters worse. I have lost more points by stubbornness in refusing to settle for a small loss than by any other one misdemeanor. Don't be afraid to consolidate a fifth as against holding out for a possible but very dubious first. If you accept fifth at an early stage of a race that was fluky enough to drop you to that position, it

BACARDI CUP

No. 5634 must bear off quickly, or else she will fall astern even more quickly.

may well be fluky enough to lift you up a few slots before the end of the day. Besides, a fifth is not the end of the world; in fact it looks mighty good after you have finished fifteenth. From a race of 1973:

"It was not clear to me until near the end of the leg that north was doomsville, and as soon as I found that out we belted all the way south, but meantime 25, 38, and 31 had got there before us and we rounded *W* fifth, with 44 way ahead, then the above three, *Flame,* one more behind us, and then a long gap because the rest of the fleet had gone more to the north. There was a gradual shift of 10–15 degrees toward the south on the way up that leg, and I think we sailed it fairly well by not turning north on the first of the header but sticking it out and being willing to cross close under the boys in order to stay in the top six."

I can hear you saying, "Let's just slow down a minute. Go back a page or two to where you said 'The answer is to go the right way.' How in blazes am I supposed to know the right way from the wrong way?" Well, I wish I could tell you; but if I could so could everyone else, there would be no choice on any windward leg, and half the challenge of the race would evaporate. I am told that there are areas where the wind blows so strong and steady that there is no preferred tack, it's just a matter of driving her to windward, and the boat that is the best conditioned, has the best sails, and is handled most efficiently gets to the first mark first. I am not sure that such conditions really exist anywhere; but if they do the racing there must be a bit boring.

On Long Island Sound the wind patterns and shifts are almost as elusive and hard to predict as they are on a small mountain lake. I have tried to keep records of the major changes during races for many years; but they don't seem to do me much good. One bit of folklore to which I do not subscribe is that there is less wind in this area than formerly. You hear people say, "There used to be fine racing breezes all summer." That just isn't so. The first year I kept any records was 1936. The accompanying table summarizes the breezes on race days for the last half of the 1936 season and most of 1937, all on western Long Island Sound. The last two available seasons are May 10–September 6, 1973 and May 20–September 29, 1974. During these two summers, in a total of 83 race days we had 11 cancellations because of calms, 34 breezes that could be called light or very light, and 38 relatively good to excellent racing breezes of 10 knots or more. This looks very like the 1930s.

| **1936, JULY 11–SEPT. 20** | | **1937, MAY 30–SEPT. 18** | |
|---|---|---|---|
| E | 4–10 knots | S | Medium–light |
| E | Light, then strong | SW | Light |
| NE | 15 | NW | Light fluky |
| E | Light, SW at 5:10 | W | Fluky, then medium SW |
| | Canceled | E | Strong |
| Calm | Then light SE | | Canceled |
| E | 20 | E | Light |
| SW | 10–20 | Various | calms and squalls |
| W | Light, then light SW | SE | Very light; late SW |
| W | 4–10 | S-SE | Very light |

| | |
|---|---|
| **NW** | Light; then SW |
| | Canceled |
| **E** | 8 |
| **SW** | 8–10 |
| **S** | Medium to light |
| **SE-S-SW** | Very light |
| **S** | 4–6 |
| **W** | 15–18 |
| **E** | Light |
| **S** | Medium–strong |
| **W** | 6–12 |
| **E** | Light; then S |
| | Canceled |
| **SW** | 8 |
| **S** | 12 |
| **NW** | Light fluky |
| **S** | 8–10 |
| **E** | Light |
| **SW** | Light; then medium W |
| **SE** | Light; then NW |
| **E** | Light; then medium S |
| **E** | 10 knots, then S, then E |
| **E** | 10, to weak S |
| **W** | Late medium S |
| **SW** | 15 |
| **S** | 15–18 |
| **SE** | Very light |
| | Canceled |
| **E to S** | Very light |
| | Canceled |
| **SE** | Light to very light |
| **S** | Medium, then NW flukes |
| **E** | Light, then N, then strong E |
| **N and W** | Very light |
| **N** | Light |
| **SE** | Light; then SW at 5:00 |

There does, however, seem to be a trend away from southwesters—which in this area really blow from about 210°, so I will call them southerlies. If the old-timers are bewailing the partial disappearance of the "prevailing southerlies," they may be right. In 1973 and 1974 combined we sailed only ten races in what could be called "standard" southerlies, the rest of the good winds coming from other directions. But it must also be remembered that in the old days many of those southerlies came up too late, around four or five o'clock, just as they do today.

I find it hard to believe that any long-term change in the weather pattern is man-made. A popular theory proposes that the increased number of highways, apartment buildings, and the like on Long Island are responsible for a decrease in wind on the Sound, the claim being that the resulting heat produces a barrier that the southerly cannot penetrate. I don't think that this is supported by meteorological fact. No hot-air mass that I ever heard of in any part of the world acts in such a manner. Hot air does not stagnate; it rises, leaving a partial vacuum that must be filled. If the summer southerly is a thermal, then the prevailing westerly or southwester is deflected to the left and drawn inland by the air rising over the land as it is heated by the midday sun. If there were no heating of the land there would be no southerly. Increased heating should, if anything, provide stronger southerlies. But if you fly over Long Island during the summer you will find that it looks just as green as it ever did. The construction has not in fact "turned it into a desert."

The trend away from southerlies applies to the entire northeastern

United States and has nothing to do with man-made structures. My guess is that there are long-term cycles in the wind patterns, and that some day we may get more southerlies again. Meanwhile, on Long Island Sound you can expect afternoon southerlies to show up more often on hot days than on cool days. Especially in early summer and late fall the chances for a southerly are minimal. In those seasons the easterlies blow east, and the westerlies blow west, all day.

If you think that there was always a breeze in "the good old days," take a look at the newspaper reports of Long Island Sound races of the 1920s. Day after day the same story: "Another regatta spoiled by lack of wind." One can go back even to the previous century. In 1896 the first Seawanhaka Cup Regatta ran into three days of very light, almost drifting conditions during its selection trials. In *Origins and History of the Seawanhaka Corinthian Yacht Club,* W. P. Stephens commented, "While the weather had been most unsatisfactory, it was only what might be expected off Oyster Bay in August." In the same book he remarked, "With all its advantages as a yachting center, Long Island Sound has one serious drawback—the lack of wind in summer—a matter which affects all of its numerous yacht clubs alike." The sailing career on which Mr. Stephens based these observations stretched from about 1871 to the time of his death in 1946, at the age of ninety-two.

A leading skipper in our fleet once won a race by choosing the westerly tack on a certain southwest beat on which it has long been accepted practice to go south. More often than not on this particular leg the southerly side pays off with a lift off the Long Island shore. But this time my friend got over on the port tack right after the start, continued on it to the lay line, and arrived at the first mark with a comfortable lead. After the race I asked him what prompted him to make that decision. He answered readily enough, "It was obvious from the start that this was the kind of day to go west." *How* it was obvious I knew better than to ask him. To him it just was. During his racing career in this area he had absorbed enough knowledge of southwesters to have a better insight into their behavior than the rest of us. No doubt he had, partly subconsciously, weighed very carefully all the evidence of wind, clouds, temperature, humidity, visibility—those factors that contribute to what the racing man calls "the feel of the day"—before arriving at the conclusion that the signals mostly pointed west. He might have been wrong, of course; no one is right every time. But it wasn't just luck. He had more to go on than the toss of a coin.

Gold medalist Buddy Melges puts it well: "I have no rule of thumb concerning tactics. They are all done on impression when in the open sea. This feel cannot be explained; but it is right more times than it is wrong." We ordinary mortals are wrong about as often as we are right; but when the balance begins to tip in your favor, you are on the way up.

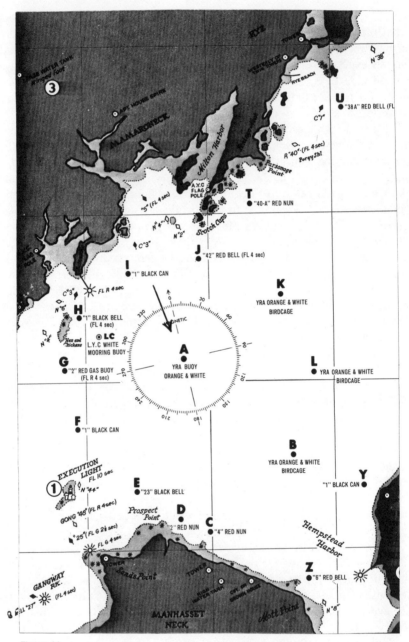

**Figure 11**

Decisions do not always have to be based on tenuous indications and gossamer wisps of uncertain evidence. Sometimes the handwriting on the wall—or to be more specific, on the signal board—is very clear. If you are tired of reading about how well we do things on the *Flame,* here is an example of how badly we do things. The entry is for June 22, 1974.

"Why do I have to keep making it so hard for us? We finished 16th today. The first mark was H, which they changed to G, and then a few minutes later put it back to H again [see chart, Figure 11]. What message does that carry? *Now* it tells me plainly that the wind had shifted from H to G, then back to H. I knew that; they were changing correctly. Then why in heaven's name didn't I realize that it would probably tend to swing back toward G [the west] after our start? But it never got through my noggin, and I set out toward the north. The race was over (for us) in about the first ten minutes: the westerly tack had a rail-down breeze and lift while we were floundering. *Flame* rounded the first mark a bad last while the leaders were rounding the second mark."

How heavily to rely on the local weather forecast depends on the area you sail in. The winds in some localities are quite predictable and the weather bureau knows accurately when a change will occur, especially if it is associated with a weather front. But where I race on the U.S. East Coast, the wind forecasts must be taken with many grains of salt, especially in summer when the weather systems become sluggish and tend to stall out. Almost as often as not the forecast can lead you astray. "After the race" [of August 21, 1971], "it went all the way around to northwest, with rain and a semi-thundersquall [whatever that means]. If this sort of thing had happened on the second windward leg, when we were pushing the southerly tack, it would have been curtains. I didn't think enough about northerlies because the forecast had said southwest. Hmmm . . ."

Hmmm, indeed. That is a good note on which to end the chapter. The problems of race strategy, the master plan for the day, whether and how much to modify that plan as the situation changes, the instant evaluation of new conditions, and what action to take to meet them, all require decisions based on careful analysis and years of experience. A strong back is of no help in this department. It is one of the more delicate, perhaps the most difficult, and certainly a very fascinating aspect of racing.

# [7]
# THE WINDWARD LEG: TACTICS

Many average to good racing skippers have what could be called a covering complex. If they cross ahead of a boat, especially a good one, anywhere on a windward leg, they flop on top of her "to cover." Sometimes they even do this shortly after the start when the two boats in question are somewhere down in mid-fleet. The skipper who thinks he is covering at that stage of the race is wasting a tack, because the victim can't take it and must simultaneously tack away to get clear. In order to avoid making too many enemies I usually look to leeward first and deliberately try to time my tacks early in the race in such a way that I do *not* smother the next nearest boat. Let him go peacefully on his way and you stand a better chance of his doing the same for you next time. If you are approaching a windward mark or the finish line, that is a different story, and no holds are barred; but early in the race you have much more important things to think about.

Contestants in a local fleet race have a weapon not available in a championship affair that brings together strangers from many different regions. In your home fleet you soon learn who are the cover fanatics and who are not, and can plan accordingly. Some will desperately cover at every opportunity, whereas others would not think of covering anything lower than third, and not even that until approaching the finish line. It makes a difference in trying to keep clear air if you have some idea of what the opposition is likely to let you do.

Sooner or later you are going to find yourself in the unhappy position of boat *A* in Figure 12, having used up all your starboard tacks. You are fetching a windward mark which, through some vagary of the local conditions, is best approached along the port

US 116 will have to tack away, probably the sooner the better.

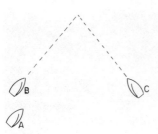

**Figure 12**

lay line. Boat *B* has just tacked all over you, and you are considering one more desperation hitch to get clear even though it will make you overstand. But if another boat, *C*, is approaching on starboard, hang on a moment longer and you may get a reprieve. Some skippers are so carried away by the power of the starboard tack that they never forego an opportunity to force a port-tack boat about, even when to do so is a tactical error. If *C*'s skipper is such a starboard-tack addict and is on collision course with *B*, you can predict what will happen. He will freeze onto that tiller and start hollering "Starboard," never noticing that, by tacking himself, he could lay the mark. *B* is loath to bear off around *C*'s transom, partly because of your presence and partly because he can't believe that *C* is going through with it. But *C* is deadly serious, and once solidified, nothing short of dynamite is going to move him. He will run perfect interference for you, putting *B* about and opening a clear path for you to the mark.

If *B* sees the light in time, he may elect to duck under *C*'s stern, in which case you will have to give him room to do so if you are overlapped. *C* ranks as an obstruction to both of you. (See NAYRU appeals 114 and 131.)

Even when you are in a logical position to protect your lead, don't get so wrapped up in covering that you forget everything else. We lost a race not long ago by making exactly this mistake.

"Just as we rounded mark *M,* the southwest wind konked to almost nothing. We then had to set about covering No. 45 for the remaining half-mile to the finish, which we thought would be easy. In a way it

Hanging in the balance: the leeward boat may just miss or just gain a safe leeward position.

was, *but;* the race had a message which we failed to read: watch the rest of the fleet too! They were so far back at $M$ that we forgot about them—an expensive little forget. They tacked south, picked up a fine breeze, and we saw them too late. We immediately headed over there, but three of them had us at the finish. That we still had 45 was some consolation, but it would have been pleasant to get boats in between. I have never seen a southwester behave quite this way in the middle of the Sound." Never mind the excuses, Skipper.

In describing the regatta that had the shorthanded committee and the poor course in Chapter 4, I indicated that the race was over at the first mark. That was not strictly true. The course was *JKD* (see Figure 11), starting and finishing at $A,$ the complete mark sequence being *AJKDJDA*. The distance from $D$ to $J$ is three miles, but today it was not dead to windward but almost a fetch on port. The arrow in Figure 11 shows the approximate wind direction. Everyone had to be very sparing with starboard tacks. We covered the second boat comfortably enough until, about three-quarters of the way up the leg, her skipper, tired of doing nothing, tacked to starboard. But he did this at just the wrong moment, on a slight port lift that pointed the *Flame* so nearly toward the mark that it would have been a waste to tack with him, especially since the wind was almost sure to come back. It was a made-to-order illustration of when not to cover. Some minutes later the wind did come back so that we were no longer fetching *J*. We then tacked, and had doubled our previous lead when we arrived at the mark.

On the return trip down to *D* nothing happened, but then came another and final windward leg of the same lopsided kind from *D* to the finish. This time different tactics were called for. There is no point in building up any more lead on the last leg; the important thing is to hold on to your place. Winning by two seconds is exactly as good as, usually better than, winning by two minutes. Some boats had taken a short starboard tack early in the leg while we aimed toward the finish line on port. We were acutely conscious of what was going on up over our shoulder astern, and eventually tacked as a safety precaution, taking a hitch in order to plant ourselves between those boats and the finish. We had to abandon the No. 2 boat to do this; but by that time it seemed to us that the new group was threatening. The second-place skipper considered this a golden chance to do what we had done on the previous round, and kept going on port. Ironically, the wind double-crossed him; he sailed into a light spot, and not only *Flame* but another boat of the windward group beat him across the finish line. The time to gamble for higher stakes is not near the finish, when it is better to cover second, but early in the race when, if you fail, time remains to recoup your loss. Approaching *J* we made a move that doubled our lead; approaching the finish under the same conditions we made exactly the opposite move, throwing away half our lead in order to guarantee any lead at all.

The race of September 3, 1972, contains enough interesting odds and ends to make it perhaps worth reproducing the entire story. We had finished fifth the day before due to bad sailing and general mismanagement. Bubbles Shattuck was the skipper who stood second in the score whenever he wasn't first, and whom we finally edged out for the season partly as a result of this last race.

"After yesterday I was in there fighting, instead of being on the eternal defensive against Bubbles and the score. It felt like a new start in life: we were out there to win, to recover. We were the aggressor. What a wonderful difference! It was immediately more fun, and I think also it must have contributed something to our success. Today it was go for broke, and it turned out to be one of the best races of

ELMON C. MORRISON

No, No. 15, you can't do that. It is a common foul to try to squeeze in from the port tack with no right to do so.

the summer, maybe *the* best. By the greatest of good luck one of the regulars who was supposed to have been away turned up, giving us a total of four aboard. The breeze was north again, almost the same direction as yesterday, but behaving this time like a northwester, not steady but with shifts to work on, and strong: at times over 25, usually 15–20.

"Made a too-good start, almost over early. We tacked only once, on a header that then aimed us for the mark. The boats were pointing so high on this short leg, with smooth water, that there was danger of overstanding on both tacks. As we continued toward the mark on port, No. 38 (Peter Cooper) and I think 40 (Paul Gooding) came along on starboard but elected to tack off our lee bow. We were able to work a bit higher than they, and just before the mark a pronounced private offshore lift put us ahead of them both. Meanwhile No. 77 came from somewhere and crossed ahead of us, laying the mark and preparing to round; but just short of the mark her spinnaker came out of the basket and filled in the water for a very efficient sea anchor, and we rounded first.

"Nobody set for a while, heading high on the close reach. One by one we all hoisted, about off Delancey Point, and *Flame* seemed to be building up a small lead; but just as we reached the mark, the bell outside Larchmont Harbor, Gooding came roaring up on a puff, Bob Walden shrieking with glee, and almost had an overlap at the bell. I had no choice but to jibe sharply and it took two on the foredeck to get the pole around and set. We managed to pull out, and ran down the long leg to *D*, Bubbles steaming along in third place but not gaining.

"Rounding *D*, Paul Gooding's spinnaker wouldn't come down. It didn't take Walden long to clear it, but meanwhile they had dropped some distance. On the long windward leg we tried to cover Bubbles loosely while at the same time paying attention to the shifts. At one stage we were sailing on port with him quite a distance to leeward directly abeam. Suddenly a strong header, so we both have to tack, and now he is to windward, astern but not very damned far astern. With much more assurance than I really felt, I remarked to the boys, 'Don't worry, it will have to come back'; and it did. Furthermore, before it had come back all the way he tacked away, so that the next time we were much farther ahead. Earlier in August I probably would have tacked to cover at the worst possible time (on the lift), and thrown away most of our lead.

"On all this starboard tack, down below us on the New Rochelle side are two or three, including Cooper, who may cross us if it heads the least bit more. However there is nothing we can do about that, eventually *J* turns up and we round first, Cooper a close second and Gooding third. Second disaster for Paul: his spinnaker halyard shackle broke, the sail went forward and under the boat and came up in five pieces. Even Walden couldn't fix that. They hoisted another, but of course by that time Bubbles had bubbled by them, which we didn't like to see because we thought they could probably have held him off.

"The second run to *D* went rapidly in so much breeze and we about held relative positions. The beat back to the finish was uneventful because Peter covered Bubbles tack for tack, making our cover automatic also. Toward the end we took it a little easy so as not to strain anything, thereby losing some of our lead but not enough to notice. Nothing busted, and the four in crew were a lifesaver."

Sometimes tacking to keep in phase with a shifty breeze can be interwoven with tacking to cover. Suppose that two boats, for whatever reason, are concerned only with each other and not with the rest of the fleet. Approaching position 1 in Figure 13, Boat *A* has a considerable lead over boat *B* in the old wind. In order to protect this lead after the shift, she can tack at $A_1$, so that when the wind phases back again she will regain her former lead. For a much larger gain, however, *A* should continue on port, sailing in the header, until she can tack right on top of *B* at position 2. *A* has now lost nearly all her lead; but *B* has no option but to tack away, onto

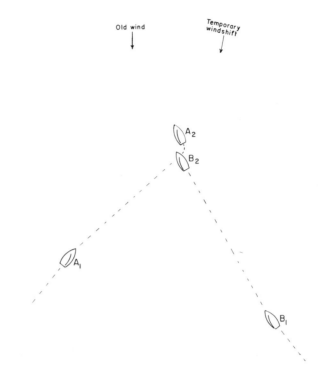

**Figure 13**

the port (headed) tack. *A* now rides out the rest of the lift on starboard, and when they meet again after the next shift *A* will be far ahead.

An interesting sort of converse to the last maneuver is illustrated in Figure 14. Here the two boats are approaching on collision course until at position 1 a small shift heads *A* and lifts *B*. The immediate reaction on board *A* is to tack at once, both to avoid passing astern of *B* and to take advantage of the header. "But if I do that," reasons *A*'s skipper, "*B* will be ahead, and the very best we can hope for is to come out even again if the wind goes back to where it was. On the other hand if I hold on this bad (port) tack and cross under *B*, I don't think he can resist the opportunity of trying a cover. He will therefore tack on top of us ($B_2$), at which moment, if we go about also ($A_2$), he may let us go. Then he will be on the wrong (headed) tack and we will be on the right (let-up) tack as we separate."

I am not making this up. Boat *A* was *Flame,* and it all worked out exactly as predicted. Of course we had to be pretty good mind readers to know just how *B* was going to react; but if you race against a pet competitor all summer you become familiar with his racing style and behavior. It is one of the few occasions on which we invented a ploy on the spur of the moment and actually pulled it off.

CHRIS CASWELL

No. 7629 has a reef rolled in; the "slab reef" was not yet in use in 1971. There was no collision. Telephoto lenses often foreshorten distance.

On another occasion we were short-tacking up a windward leg, unsuccessfully attempting to catch the boat ahead. When he finally let us go, I in my enthusiasm overstood the starboard lay line. As we approached the mark he was still ahead, coming across on port. He could have tacked far away from us and laid the mark with ease; but he was so fascinated with "covering" that he waited until he was close aboard and then tacked under our lee bow (at $B_1$, Figure 15). By now he was overstanding also, and had thus tossed away part of his lead; but worse than that, it was necessary to tack around the mark, leaving it to starboard, to head for the finish. We were not overlapped at the mark; but he was so close that he could not tack until we did, which put us ahead at position 2. I might add that he was not one of the world's greatest skippers, or he would not have made such an obvious error. We were battling it out for about fifth place in a rather minor race. But I don't refuse any gift, even if it is only a fifth.

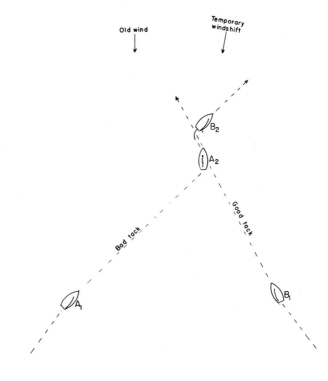

Old wind

Temporary
windshift

B₂

A₂

Good tack

Bad tack

A₁

B₁

**Figure 14**

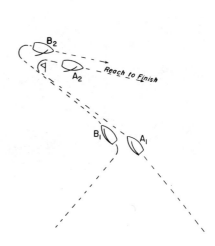

Wind

B₂

A₂

Reach to Finish

B₁

A₁

**Figure 15**

MARINE GRAPHICS, SAN DIEGO

*Bullseye* tried to hang in there, but of course it could not be. By pinching the least bit, US 171 was able to force *Bullseye* to drop off to leeward and try to sail around.

Probably the most famous example of a mistaken attempt to cover cost the challenger *Endeavour* the third race and perhaps the America's Cup in 1934. She had won the first two, and three down with one to go would have been a tough position for even Harold Vanderbilt to escape from. The course was leeward-windward, fifteen miles downwind with supposedly a fifteen-mile beat back to the finish, and *Endeavour* rounded the leeward mark with a *six-and-a-half-minute* lead. Vanderbilt went below "to drown his sorrows in coffee and sandwiches," and brood about how it would feel to be the first American ever to lose the cup. When he came on deck fifteen minutes later the whole picture had changed.

The wind had hauled so far during the first leg that the last leg was not a true beat but a close fetch on the starboard tack. This made the situation especially grim for *Rainbow,* but Sherman Hoyt, at the helm, did not give up. Instead he held even higher, deliberately overstanding the finish in the hope of luring *Endeavour* into making exactly the mistake she did make. *Endeavour* was still a long way ahead and in the right place, virtually between her opponent and the finish, but in the light of what happened next it would appear that at least some of those aboard *Endeavour* did not think so at the time. She sailed into a soft spot and slowed down, and there was *Rainbow,* beginning to loom larger on the weather quarter. Vanderbilt wrote that he "could see the returning breeze rippling the water" some distance ahead of the challenger. Sopwith, being much nearer to it, must have seen it too. Even so, he tacked. There was a slight haze, and the probable explanation for *Endeavour*'s tack is that they were not sure where the finish was and thought that the leg was still a beat to windward.

It took *Endeavour* a long time to get going on the port tack in the light air, and then she made a second error. Instead of tacking under *Rainbow*'s lee bow and well ahead of her, she crossed *Rainbow* and tried to execute a direct smother cover. The two boats were much too close for that, and *Rainbow* easily sailed through *Endeavour*'s lee. Sopwith then tacked *again* (more distance sailed away from the finish line,) and *Rainbow* went on to win the race by three minutes, never having tacked at all. In fact they had to ease sheets before the end of the leg.

Vanderbilt did not know about the plot that Sherman Hoyt was hatching while he, Vanderbilt, was below having lunch; it came out much later in Hoyt's memoirs. But plot or no plot, as Vanderbilt remarked drily, "It can be said in all fairness that, from a tactical standpoint, it seldom pays to try to get in position to tack on another boat's wind, when, in order to attain that position, you have to sail for 5 minutes with the finish line, still 10 miles away, bearing at least a point aft of your beam" (*On the Wind's Highway*).

For another example of inveigling the opposition into making an error, we dip once more into ancient history to see how Arthur Knapp won the World's Championship of the Star Class in 1930 on Chesapeake Bay. With the last race of a five-race series remaining to be sailed, Walton Hubbard was leading Knapp by two points, with the third boat six points farther back. The day of the final race produced a full-scale northeaster blowing 20 to 25 knots. It was the first year of the Star's "new rig," with a tall mast and sail plan, and no one knew much about what it would do in a blow. Whether for this reason or not, a few boats in that last race, including the two leaders, were reefed down. The course was three times around a triangle (with a downwind start!). At the end of two rounds Hubbard was fifth and Knapp seventh, and it looked as if the championship was on its way back to California where Hubbard had taken it once before. Then, before arriving at the last leeward mark, Knapp took an inspired if somewhat desperate step: he shook out his reef. The wind was blowing even harder; but Arthur already had proof that he couldn't catch Hubbard unless he took drastic measures, and he had to hope that Hubbard would follow suit. He had no assurance that he could handle full sail any better than Hubbard could, but he knew that if he didn't try *something* he was through. The gambit worked and Hubbard shook out also, following the maxim, "When in the lead, do what your principal opponent is doing." One by one Knapp passed boats on that final windward leg while Hubbard was losing them, to finish five boats ahead for an eleventh-hour series victory.

On very rare occasions it is the leading boat that must practice deception. Perhaps the most spectacular decoy on record was successfully executed by Peter Bordes in a race of the Thistle Class Nationals. The launch that set the first windward mark left the starting area on the warning gun and disappeared into a blinding downpour with lightning and thunder. No one was sure exactly where it had gone or whether it would come to roost in the right place when the wind settled down after the squall; but the race was started on time anyway, because the committee had a very sick man aboard who had to be put ashore without delay. (Race procedure often hinges on extraneous problems of which the contestants are entirely unaware.) The wind had been blowing from the east, parallel to the shore; but during the squall it shifted substantially toward the northeast, so that now the starboard tack carried the boats almost straight toward the beach and the port tack almost parallel to the beach. They sailed to windward for a while, and before long the shoreline loomed up ahead out of the murk, still with no mark in sight. The fleet did the natural thing: they kept on sailing east, mostly on port, farther and farther up the beach. Bordes finally became convinced that they had all sailed beyond the mark; that it could no longer be to the eastward but must in fact be west of the place where they had originally sighted land. He was a local, and a past champion, and he guessed (correctly) that the others thought he knew where he was and were more or less following him. What to do? If he turned and ran west the fleet, to the west of him, would do likewise and he would be last instead of first. He and his crew, on the spur of the moment, manufactured a brilliant solution: *they faked a broken main halyard* and let the sail come tumbling down. While they made a show of frantically trying to get it up again, the entire fleet sailed past, doubtless offering sympathetic suggestions. When everybody had safely gone by, Peter calmly re-hoisted and set a spinnaker. It all worked according to plan: the fleet did follow, the mark did eventually appear down the coast to the west, and Bordes went on to win the race and subsequently the series.

# [8]
# SPINNAKER TECHNIQUES

Spinnakers can be hoisted in a wide variety of different ways. Once upon a time they were sent up in stops. Now the stops have become rubber bands on larger boats and have been eliminated entirely on small boats. Spinnakers have been hoisted out of boxes, bags, bins, and baskets. Some boats have built-in chutes or tubes into which the sail disappears as it comes down, all ready for instant re-hoisting, untouched by human hands on the round trip. These tubes have mostly been prohibited on bigger boats, partly because they sometimes take aboard large quantities of water. In some keel-boat classes the present vogue is to pack the spinnaker in a rectangular plastic wastebasket that is snapped onto the lee shrouds shortly before hoisting time.

We are currently working on a variant that has served us well: we rig the basket inside the cockpit instead of on the lee shrouds. There are attachments for the basket in both bilges, so we still have to choose the correct side. Once that is done the sheets are made fast to the sail and all is in readiness except the halyard, which goes on immediately before hoisting. No awkward basket has to be carried up and snapped to the shrouds just when things are getting critical at the end of the windward leg; no rush to attach the sheets; no necessity for someone to hold the sail against its prematurely blowing out of the basket; and finally, a tactical advantage that did not occur to me until we had begun to use this procedure: you automatically conceal your plans from the competition, instead of having to advertise in advance which jibe you have selected. The only disadvantage to date is that the sail doesn't go up quite so easily. Close synchronization is required between the hoister and the man on the guy to get that guy around

TOM WITHERSPOON, LONG BEACH NEWS
Somebody trimmed the guy before the halyard crew had it all the way up.

fast enough. On a dead run the spinnaker tends to get caught between the mainsail and the lee spreader. To avoid this, we arrange things differently when we know that the next hoist will take place on a run: we rig both sheets and the halyard forward of the main shrouds. That is to say, when the sail goes up it is led directly forward out of the cockpit, so that all three attachments and the sail itself go out under the spreader and *inside* the main shrouds. It works smoothly this way, and the sail is in a better position to fill once it is up.

Hoisting from an interior cockpit basket has made me wonder whether, except in a hard blow, there is any need to pack the spinnaker at all. Perhaps we should all be hoisting straight out of the cockpit, as they do in any small centerboarder not equipped with a tube. We haven't attempted this yet on the *Flame*.

A good spinnaker flies well in a breeze, downwind, with the outer end of the pole as high as possible. How high is that? Raise the inner end almost to the top of the slide and then let the outer end ride a foot or so above that. Certainly a horizontal pole allows the maximum spread between the two clews; but you don't lose much length with a slightly angled pole. Raising the outer end of a nine-foot pole twelve inches above the horizonal reduces its effective length by less than three-quarters of an inch, hardly an amount to cause concern. On the other hand, the added height may be quite desirable.

Some crews think that lowering the outer end of the pole flattens the sail. In fact it has the opposite effect, by tightening the leech (or luff if you prefer) on that side of the sail. The way to gain area is to let the two clews go *up,* thus allowing the leeches to open away from the middle of

A spinnaker that wants to fly usually levels the clews automatically.

F. NAKAJIMA

the sail. The whole sail then assumes a shape more like a soup plate and less like an elongated bowl. A circular perimeter contains the maximum available projected area.

Many people are too concerned about whether the two clews are riding at the same height. Forget it. They can hardly do otherwise, and will automatically adjust themselves unless the sheet is being badly over-· trimmed. Try to keep the foot of the sail well away from the jibstay at all times. If the sail is touching anything it means that either somebody is doing something wrong or there is not enough wind to carry.

In very light airs with a sloppy sea you have a problem keeping the sail filled at all, and then it may become necessary to drop the pole in order deliberately to tighten the leeches to prevent them from collapsing.

Let the mast go forward on a run by easing the backstay a lot, to help bring the three corners of the spinnaker (and of the mainsail!) more nearly into the same vertical plane. Easing the spinnaker halyard a foot or so may do the same, but it will tend to make the sail oscillate or yaw. We usually hoist all the way.

The crew is often uncertain exactly how much to trim or ease the after guy. Probably the pole should be square to the apparent wind. In determining that angle, a small yarn or ribbon telltale fastened to the topping lift just above its attachment to the pole may be of more help than the masthead fly. It works better than you'd expect it to.

When a jibe goes wrong everyone blames the foredeck crew. Actually it is much more the fault of the skipper and the middle man. Let's assume that the jibe is from reach to reach, the only difficult kind. Whoever is tending the sheet and guy must understand that it is *his* responsibility to keep the sail filled. This means that he must let the old sheet very far forward in mid-jibe to prevent the sail from falling into the fore-triangle. It is the skipper's obligation to turn the boat slowly underneath the full spinnaker. The "slowly" is the mickey. In a hairy jibe at a crowded mark the skipper cannot help the spinnaker crew. They are on their own to do the best they can under adverse conditions. Any good crew gladly accepts the challenge and delights in vying with the crews of the other boats, who are all in the same trouble, in getting set on the new jibe. If there is time to jibe at leisure, always swing wide of the mark, trim the main all the way in, and hold the boat dead before it until they are reorganized on the new side. With the wind thus allowed to flow past both sides of the mainsail into the spinnaker, they have no trouble in keeping it from breaking. When both skipper and crew are working to turn the boat under the sail the whole jibing operation becomes almost automatic, and you begin to pick up boats instead of dropping them at each rounding. I have seen a foredeck man clutching vainly for the (old) sheet in order to snap it into the pole when a 10° turn of the hull would put it right in his hand.

On most boats the foreguy goes to some point well forward on the deck. We prefer to lead it down vertically, to a point only a few feet for-

Much can be gained or lost at the jibing mark.

ward of the mast. To be sure, the pole is not so firmly held from this position; but the advantage is that you can make quite sizable adjustments on the after guy (which seems to be happening all the time on our boat), without touching the foreguy. We changed it once, to see how it would work farther forward, and everybody immediately demanded its return to the old position. What the pole loses in horizontal stability it gains in vertical stability. That is, if the foreguy leads too far forward a very small vertical component remains to keep the pole from skying. On some boats it has been found necessary to control the lead angle of the after guy by means of a fairlead or hook on deck in way of the cockpit to provide sufficient downpull on the pole. This is entirely obviated by a "straight-down" foreguy. Finally, you get an extra dividend because of the jib sheets. If the foreguy's point of attachment on deck is far enough aft, the guy can be set up between the two sheets so that the jib is always ready for trimming on either tack without any frantic changing over.

On the *Flame* we are seldom quite as ready for the downwind leg as we should be before arriving at the windward mark. Interest and excitement run high in the last few minutes of a windward leg, and it is sometimes hard to remember to "do all the things": slack the main outhaul, raise the gooseneck, set the vang, slack the backstay, attach the spinnaker halyard. The middle man should be taking care of these items while the foredeck hand is getting his pole forward and rigged. If your crew can do all this smoothly and quickly, allowing you to sail serenely on, thinking only about how best to approach the mark, you have made more progress on the road to efficient operation than we have achieved on the *Flame*.

After rounding, don't be in too great a hurry to hoist. You may want to seek clear air first, well off to one side if someone is on your transom. Or if the leg is a reach you may not have decided whether you want to hoist

F. NAKAJIMA

Now what? The spinnaker was hoisted before the foredeck man was anything like ready for it (the pole is not attached to anything). Better get it down again—but *not* before letting go the forward clew and gathering in like mad from the other clew.

at all. Sail slightly high of the course, look the situation over, and then bear away and hoist if that is what the conditions call for. It goes without saying that you first consult the compass; you must know exactly where the next mark is.

If the second leg of a triangle is a close reach without spinnakers, the third leg is usually a run on the opposite jibe. You must then decide whether to hold high, set the spinnaker, and jibe around the mark, or hold off and set after rounding. The decision is sometimes made for you because you have everything rigged for a set on the reaching leg and don't want to change it all to the other side with the boat on her beam ends.

On a reach in a breeze the whole crew should be on the windward rail as soon as the spinnaker is up and drawing. They are usually too concerned about getting the jib down. It is quite possible that you want to leave it up, so don't rush that move. See what the others are doing first. We have mostly been leaving jibs up on reaches and lowering them on runs, but procedures vary with circumstances. If you are trying to point as high as you can with the spinnaker in light air, be sure that the jib is down. The jib filled on a close reach will suck the spinnaker up against its lee side and collapse the whole sail. One or the other of them must be down under these conditions.

Some people think that a working jib can do some good acting as a tallboy on a dead run. I doubt if it helps any. Indeed, it is entirely possible that under certain conditions the boat would go fastest under spinnaker alone, with even the mainsail down. I haven't tried that yet, but it just might work.

Running dead before it is almost a thing of the past, except in a very heavy wind. If you are up to hull speed or planing, as the case may be, you want the shortest course to the mark even if it is dead downwind. Under any other conditions it nearly always pays to "tack downwind," the added distance being more than offset by the increase in speed. This is more important in high-aspect-ratio boats than low, and is especially apparent in light airs with leftover seas or power-boat slop. You can afford to go 30° high of the course if doing so will pick up your speed 16 percent.

The spinnaker pole appears to be too skyed; but then again, nothing is normal on these Australian 18-footers.

PROFESSIONAL YACHT PHOTOS

We were asking this spinnaker to do the impossible. It should have been sheeted much farther forward; and besides, it was too new for close reaching (the center pleat had not yet worked itself out).

Under the right conditions, 30° from dead before it will increase the speed far more than 16 percent, and a greater course deviation makes for still more speed through the water. However, you should be wary of taking the boat from a position that was not dead to windward of the mark to a position that is dead to windward of it. The downwind leg becomes a fascinating game of jibing back and forth, each skipper experimenting with how far to go and at what angle. Somebody overdoes it and gets left behind; somebody else gauges it just right. And occasionally the lone stalwart who sails straight for the mark without any jibing gets there first after all. Everything depends on the conditions, and no two leeward legs are completely alike.

In real drifting or almost drifting conditions, when you have changed down to the lightest sheets and the crew is having trouble keeping the sail drawing at all, the best thing to do is to try to keep moving. In other words, do *something;* don't just sit there and wait for wind. Try to get the boat going, in any direction, even if it is ridiculously far off course. You are shortening the distance to the mark, if only slightly; and by sailing away from where you were becalmed you can't do worse and may do better. Don't worry now about putting yourself in a position dead to weather of the mark: by the time you get there on such a day as this the wind will have shifted again. Sailing high on a broad reach on a windy day is risky

An hourglass, or has it accidentally been hoisted behind a shroud? In either case, the point is not so much how to fix it, but rather that it should not have happened in the first place.

because you have to pay for it while coming back down, but on a very light day the boats that hold off and suffer while others go by to windward are usually cheated out of their reward.

The cruising-racing classes, with their large sail inventories, have all kind of floaters, drifters, flankers, spankers, star-cuts, and other quasi-spinnakers especially designed for reaching, particularly in light weather. Even without any of these special-purpose sails, a modern small keel boat with an ordinary spinnaker can carry higher on the wind than used to be the custom. Of course whenever the spinnaker is full it *seems* to be doing a lot of work, even though it may be only heeling the boat over and pushing it sideways. Sometimes the fleet leaves them up too long, until some brave soul lowers and begins to creep out ahead with the jib. But before that stage is reached, to make the spinnaker work to its maximum you must understand that it is playing the role of a genoa jib. The pole must be carried much lower than on a run, to straighten the luff, and even the sheet may need to be lowered. No genoa could be trimmed to the transom. If the spinnaker sheet is led all the way aft under these close reaching conditions, the clew will ride too high, the whole top of the sail will turn into a sack, and you will find that the sheet tender has the foot badly overtrimmed in an unsuccessful attempt to control the rest of the sail. The remedy is to choke off the sheet by snubbing it to some point on deck in the approximate vicinity of the helmsman, and then ease it as much as it will take.

Everything must be re-tooled for the next beat *before* arriving at the end of the downwind leg. It is particularly annoying to find, after rounding the leeward mark, that the outhaul is not right and that nobody remembered to center the main traveler. A main outhaul rigged with a high mechanical advantage can be adjusted on the wind, but such an adjustment is not recommended in a breeze: it puts too much tension on the clew because of the heavy friction in the bolt rope groove, and can actually tear the clew out of the sail. If you get into this predicament, ease the mainsheet momentarily during the hauling-out process. But whatever you do, *don't* sail the whole windward leg with the outhaul too slack.

The windward takedown has for some time been popular among the centerboarders, and has been used neatly and successfully in a few larger keel boats. It is useful only at the end of a dead run, not a reach. The after guy must be released from the pole, presumably after detaching the pole and bringing it inboard. Then as the halyard is lowered the sheet is let fly instead of the guy. The advantage is that the sail falls on deck or into the cockpit almost of its own accord, with much less danger of its dragging overboard. It must be fed aft under the windward spreader, and therefore the pins and cotters up there must be carefully checked for jagged protrusions that might tear the sail. A nicely executed windward takedown is a "now you see it, now you don't" operation: the sail disappears as if by magic. The resident magicians on the *Flame* do not have it down pat yet, but they are working on it.

Most crews are eager to get the boat tidied up for the windward leg immediately after rounding. This is the wrong time to tidy. As soon as the pole is stowed, forget everything except getting the boat trimmed and moving. Someone should check that there are no spinnaker sheets dragging overboard, and then all crew should immediately scramble out to windward if it is breezing on. None of that dreadful-looking mess in the bilge is doing any harm there. Only one man should clean it up, and he can do it any time. Leave the heaviest part of the crew on the rail and let whoever is best at sneaking around the boat quietly and unobtrusively straighten things out *after* you have settled down. If the spinnaker has to be re-packed, let him do it two-thirds of the way up the windward leg. By that time the weather may be calmer and you will be too. If this is a beat to the finish, just push the sail forward out of the way and forget it. There is one exception: on a light fluky day always have some spinnaker ready to go up, even if you think there is no more downwind work left in the race. You never can tell. Also *never* strip the sheets off the deck until you have crossed the finish line.

Occasionally in middle-distance racing and even sometimes in day racing the following rather odd situation can arise. You are approaching a mark on a beam reach, just able to carry the spinnaker. After rounding, the course to the next mark will be such that you anticipate being able to carry again, on the other jibe. The hitch is that through some combination of circumstances the mark is not a jibing mark; you must leave it to windward. That is, you must tack around it. What to do?

You might be tempted, especially if you fail to plan ahead and are suddenly confronted with the unusual rounding, to tack around the mark allstanding, with the spinnaker up. Don't try it. If the wind is very light the sail will plaster itself against the mast and spreaders, becoming such a brake that the boat will fail to carry through the wind's eye. And if the wind is any stronger than very light you are inviting a terrible tangle and a torn sail. The rounding should be planned far enough ahead so that you can douse the spinnaker, round under genoa or working jib, and then re-hoist on the new side. If it is beam reach to beam reach the boat will go almost as fast without the spinnaker anyway. This is an occasion on which a spinnaker chute (tube) would be a welcome assist; but in the absence of one, a good crew can get everything around and up again in short order. However, don't let them take any shortcuts. Better to take time to keep things in order than risk a foul-up.

# [9]
# DOWNWIND TACTICS

There was a time when many yachtsmen believed that the race was won or lost on the windward leg, and that the offwind legs were relatively uninteresting and usually a procession. This is not so today. A great change has been brought about by modern hulls and sail plans; and the ways to use these to best advantage are still being explored. A downwind leg, especially a dead run, can require almost as much skill and ingenuity as a beat to windward, and yield as many surprises.

If the leg is a broad reach, perhaps 30° to 40° above a dead run, the fleet tends to luff out to windward of the rhumb line (straight line to the next mark) as soon as spinnakers have been set. This can be caused by one or two boats trying to clear their air, which blankets someone ahead who has to luff in response, and a chain reaction is set off. The fleet leaders then have to make a difficult choice. They look back and see everybody luffing well out to windward and, in consequence, traveling very fast. Should they, the leaders, follow suit or hold low, on course, hoping to reap their reward later when "what goes up has to come down"? Whatever decision you make as leader must be made fast and early. If you wait until they are abeam it is probably too late: you are then committed to stay low. Unfortunately the dividends that are meant to accrue to the leeward boat are sometimes defaulted. The windward boats are certainly making better speed through the water, and if there is a major windshift they may never have to pay that back. Also they have their wind clear—that's why they went up there—and the rhumb-liner is always in bothered air. The northwester is a breeze especially treacherous to the conservative leeward boat: the windward crowd may "ride an edge" of air that never reaches the boats down below. So unless you have a handsome lead on a steady day (a rare occurrence indeed), it is safest to stay with that part of the fleet that is closest behind you, keeping a wary eye on all others if possible.

The whole group that has worked up to weather may find itself a long way to windward of the rhumb line, and the last part of the leg for those boats often becomes a dead run. Of course they don't turn and run dead before it, but they do have to get down somehow, by tacking downwind; and if the breeze is steady and blowing 10 knots or more this may be your chance to do some recovering from a bad windward leg. If you round the first mark in mid-fleet or worse, instead of following the leaders bear off straight toward the second mark or even a little below it and hope for the best. You can't win by tagging after them, and the rhumb-line course, in undisturbed air this time, may well be the best. If anything goes wrong with their calculations you will close a lot of the gap. After the race one of the erstwhile leaders will say to you, "I knew it was better down there, but I couldn't afford to stay low." It is just this delicate balance between the two options, created by the extreme responsiveness of the modern hull under a spinnaker, that has changed the downwind leg from a parade to an absorbing contest.

As you round the first (windward) mark, before the above situations even arise you have to make the more fundamental decision whether to hoist at all. If you are leading on a close reach, wait and see. This is the right time to apply the old rule: Do what the most dangerous opponent does.

"Opening day of Race Week. Everyone went pretty well south, and you had the usual guessing game as to when to tack for Prospect Bell. We missed it, but only by a few yards, No. 50 up inside us rounding first. We almost ran into his transom at the start of the reach. It was already a fine breeze on the close reach from here to *B.* All went slightly high preparatory to setting. No. 50, still leading, set first; what an error! He couldn't carry, tried desperately to, and lost five places, finally having to lower in order to fetch the mark. The rest of us thanked him for the free lesson, reached to *B,* jibed around it and then set for the next leg."

In another race we played the leading role in a comedy of errors that taught the lesson in reverse.

"June 9, 1973. The second leg was from *G,* the Larchmont outer gas-buoy, to *D* under the Long Island beach, a close-ish spinnaker reach. We did not hoist in the strong breeze, but Bubbles and Willy did immediately, of course, although behind us and apparently falling off badly. We were all quite high, so pretty soon we and Bill Ketcham in 22 decided it was time to hoist. Our spinnaker went up with a very strange knot in it that took a long time to clear, but somehow we reached along with it half up without losing too much. Finally they got it unwound and up, and although in the meantime Bubbles had gone by to leeward, the three boats up to windward were so appalled by our troubles that they did not hoist at all, and we soon passed them. By establishing an overlap on No. 22 at *D,* we managed to round a close second to Bubbles."

When the downwind leg is a true run, there is no reason to delay hoisting: get the spinnaker up as soon as you are clear of the boat astern. But in light and fluky conditions, do not become so involved in trying to get the sail set and drawing that you fail to look around you. Nature has designed us to watch out ahead but not astern. Normally I try to detail a crew member to report on everything that is going on behind us; but he is busy during the hoisting operation and it is up to me to look.

"August 15, 1971: We actually rounded second, but everybody was very bunched. As we started the final run, everything suddenly hit the fan. No. 40, sailed by someone named Dave, luffed Bubbles high (toward the east), and they got stuck in a hole. We jibed just in time but not until Isdale, sizing up the situation better than I, had sailed by on the west side of us. McMichael coming up fast astern was enough to open my eyes. 45, 40, and 52 got left out to the east and Bubbles, having led all day, finished the race 5th. We fell into line just astern of Dooie [Isdale] and just ahead of Howard [McMichael], and stayed that way to the end."

Whenever the course contains a run, you will be wondering on which jibe to set. If it really is a dead run it makes no difference. There will be much tacking downwind, and you can base your decision on the course you intend to sail. Sometimes it works the other way: the course you sail is dictated by the jibe on which you happen to set. Don't be disturbed if this happens. If you are leading and set on the starboard jibe, the chances are that the next boat or boats will either set to port or jibe immediately onto port. Your normal procedure is now to jibe also, unless you have some strong preference for the tack you are on. At least you have had a few seconds longer than they to take in the situation and weigh the advantages.

Sometimes, by some miscalculation or because of a sudden windshift at the mark, you realize too late that you are set up to hoist on what will clearly be the wrong jibe. Again, don't panic. Just proceed normally, sail fast, and make the most of this "wrong" jibe while you are on it. As soon as the crew is organized, jibe over. You are now substantially to leeward

During the next two seconds she capsized. The speed of the roll is indicated by the water cascading off the bottom.

of the rhumb line and it may look as if you have lost a boat or two; but you can probably get them back later. In all likelihood it will end up as a tacking downwind proposition, and you have merely taken one of your tacks early. The leeward berth acquired "by mistake" may be quite beneficial in the end.

The game of tacking downwind on a light and spotty run is a combination of observation, judgment, and luck, with an underlying motif of skill in keeping the boat moving. A race sailed in October 1974 illustrates some of these features. We had rounded the windward mark sixth.

"The run to *K* was interminable in the light air. First of all the leading boat took the wrong jibe from the very start, in to Westchester and oblivion. The rest of us chugged along on starboard, high to keep up steam. After a while we had not gone as high as some, and it was evident that we were never going to catch them that way, so we jibed. They soon jibed also, but not before they had run into a very soft spot, and by this time we were well on our way toward Rye. We continued to a point dead ahead of the one-time leader, now slinking back on starboard jibe, and then jibed back with him, thinking that he was none too happy with the course he was steering for the mark.

That was an error: he was *plenty* low enough, and I doubtless should have jibed a little sooner. So here we were, with the pole way forward, going fast toward the mark but annoyed at having overdone it. However, of the bunch that converged together at *K* we were the inside boat, able to round first, and simply stayed ahead for the rest of the race."

Another interesting situation developed on what my notes called "a sloppy bouncy day with a lot of power-boat waves and only about 4 knots of wind." We rounded the windward mark second with a long dead run ahead, and "elected the port jibe because the leading boat took the other jibe to cover most of the fleet." You may well ask why we didn't go with them, in an attempt to guard our second place. Perhaps we should have. But here, as in all the illustrations that I quote from *Flame*'s frequently erratic record, I am telling you what actually happened, not what you and I might agree should have happened. It would be all too easy to retouch the picture, but if I did that most of the illustrations would go out of focus. They are much more instructive as they stand. You make most of your gains in yacht racing through other skippers' errors, just as you suffer most of your losses through your own.

Meanwhile, back on the port jibe . . . The fleet split so widely that it was impossible to say who was going to be ahead when we came together again. Eventually we spotted the mark under the main boom and jibed to head for it. It now developed that the direct course for the mark was still too slow, and we had to reach high to keep up speed. As we converged with the former leader, it was evident that we were going to cross him. We expected to do one more "separate, jibe, and come back together again," in which case we would arrive at the mark outside and on the wrong jibe; but that was a chance we had to take (see Figure 16).

It turned out differently. You never know from where you sit what it looks like from the other boat. As soon as our competitor reached our wake, *he jibed*. It is easy now to see why, but I never predicted it at the time. On the other boat they thought that we had jibed at (1) to head directly for the mark, and it never occurred to them that we had had to do otherwise; so they jibed in our wake to follow us on what had looked to them to be a fast course to the mark. Now we had only to bear off and run dead before it on our starboard jibe, with the other boat just far enough astern not to bother us.

I should have guessed in advance that this would happen, and then made sure that it did. It is difficult to see from one side and astern whether another boat is exactly on course. By bearing off slowly toward the mark as the competitor came into our wake, we could have reinforced his belief that we had been heading for the mark all along, thus virtually guaranteeing that he would jibe astern of us.

Try to exploit every possibility of converting a potential gain into a

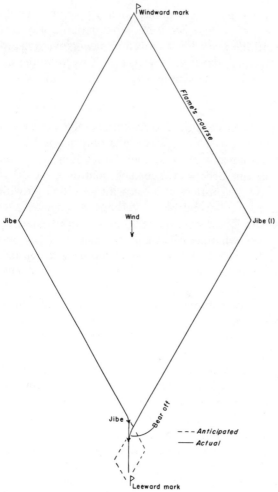

**Figure 16**

reality. Suppose you are the leeward of two boats running side by side, a few lengths apart, with the wind well abaft the beam. You feel that you have a shade more downwind speed than the other boat, but she holds you back: every time you start moving ahead you run into her wind shadow. Finally a third boat comes up astern and tries to blanket you. This is your chance to break away. By gently luffing the third boat, you may be able to feed her into a luffing match with the second boat, especially if they are both aggressive types. As soon as they get involved with each other you duck down to leeward, where their antics leave you with clear air at last. This is such a well-known ploy that boats 2 and 3 do not always take the bait. The best skippers try to avoid all luffing matches in mid-race.

A variant of this trick was played on me most successfully on a spinnaker reach into Manhasset Bay, a long bottleneck with a high bluff on the windward side (a very odd place for a race course, but there we were). The second boat, which we were trying to cover, was local and knew how to thread this maze far better than I did. Just ahead was an International One-Design, not carrying a spinnaker, which we were rapidly overtaking. By holding high, our friend astern led us neatly up to windward of the IOD. He guessed correctly that we would not dare to bear off and try to go around (although of course that is what we should have done), because of our timidity in the face of his superior local knowledge. As soon as we were safely tucked away to windward of the IOD and to leeward of the bluff, he bore away and sailed serenely around us both. It took us forever to get past the interference, and by that time the damage had been done.

As the boat astern, use every wile at your command. As the boat ahead, try to determine which moves must be countered in orthodox fashion and which are fakes, and keep one jump ahead of the game.

# [IO]
# THE LEEWARD MARK

The rounding of the leeward mark in keel boats is a very different maneuver from the same rounding in centerboarders. The smaller craft can hug the turn so tightly that the inside boat has all the advantage and there is little to be done about it: any outside overlapped boats are left astern. But in larger boats there is more to it than that. A keel boat cannot spin on a dime. It has a definite turning radius, sometimes quite large, and any tighter turn it simply cannot do. This leads to various moves and countermoves.

Of two boats side by side and bow to bow, the inside boat rounds first. Figure 17 indicates the very best possible outcome for $B$, with $A$ still in the favored position. If there are more boats overlapped outside $B$ during the approach, then $B$ may be happy to settle for second; but if the issue is only between $A$ and $B$, then $B$ should take steps to avoid being caught in position $B_1$. The standard maneuver for $B$ will work whenever $A$ is too busy lowering spinnaker, etc., to remember to make a countermaneuver, or when there is a strong following current (with the wind). Just before arriving at the mark, $B$ swings wide enough to complete most of her turn before $A$ has started hers, $B$'s bow crossing $A$'s stern very close aboard the mark (Figure 18). $A$ will come out of the turn at the positions marked (3) wondering wha' hoppen.

But they won't wonder very long, so don't expect to be able to do this twice to the same boat. Next time $A$ will try to follow $B$ out to the right and swing wide herself, to keep the relative positions of the two boats unchanged (Figure 19). Just how far away from the mark can $A$ hold $B$? The answer is, not very, because the rules require $B$ to allow $A$ room to round and no more. $B$ is usually traveling faster than $A$ at position (2), and must guard against running into $A$'s transom.

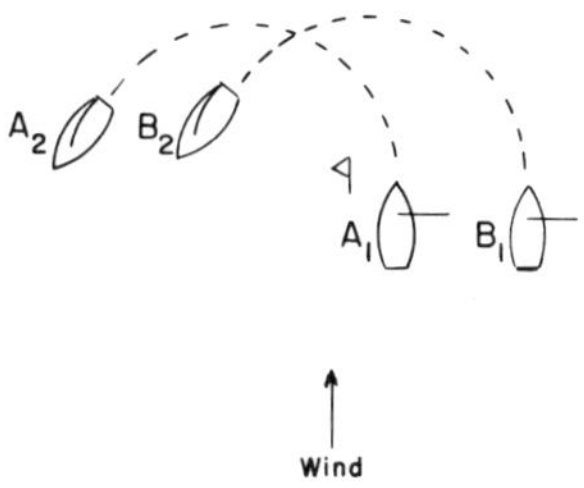

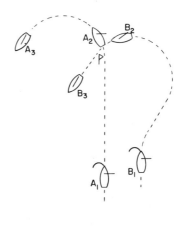

**Figure 17**

**Figure 18**

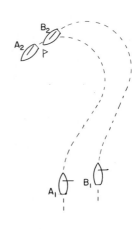

**Figure 19**

If $B$ is not overlapped as they approach, the situation is quite different. Now $A$ is under no obligation to pass the mark close aboard, and can swing as wide as she pleases to make a turn that leaves no room for anybody to pass inside her. If you are dead astern of a boat approaching the leeward mark, she will doubtless negotiate with you to establish the fact that you have no overlap outside the two-length circle. If this has been done and she then widens out, inside the circle, in order to make a good turn, don't be trapped into trying to duck inside her. You haven't a right in the world, and you will either foul out or be forced to pass on the wrong side of the mark (Figure 20).

But you still have a good defense left. In order to execute her move, Boat $A$ will have to turn as tightly as she can, sometimes overdoing it and going almost head to wind at the end. You should time things so that you sweep around outside Boat $A$ in a long smooth curve, making maximum use of reaching speed. You will thus cross her transom at a time when she is moving slowly, and you can easily break through in lee and establish yourself in a quite respectable position at $B_3$ (Figure 21).

All the above roundings presuppose that it is immaterial from a tactical point of view which tack you wish to take to begin the new windward leg. If the choice is a free one, by all means sail a few yards or a few hundred yards on the port tack. This will carry you fastest away from the area of badly disturbed air that hangs around every leeward mark, not to mention the oncoming boats. If you tack too soon you must fight your way across the wash and backwind of the rest of the fleet.

There are exceptions, the most obvious one occurring when the next leg is a close fetch on starboard, perhaps only a short leg to the finish. Now any distance sailed on the port tack is wasted. In a race at the end of last summer we made a botch of the long windward leg and arrived at the

**Figure 20**

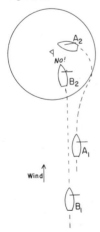

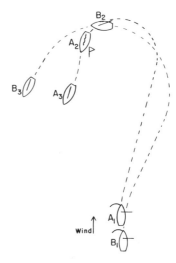

**Figure 21**

weather mark in sixth place. The boats telescoped somewhat on the run, so that at the last leeward mark we had almost caught up to the next group of three, which were all overlapped. Amid the luffing and shouting it was evident that they were slowing down when they finally bore off for the mark, as we came on fast from a leeward (outside) position. We swung wide and then aimed straight for the mark on a beam reach. The last of the three overlapped boats was now squarely in our path, but she was also the inside boat, being forced to sail so near the mark that she was not going to be able to make a good turn. We kept going and shot between her tran-

Half the crowd should tack immediately to get out of this mess, unless there is some very strong reason to head for the beach.

som and the mark as the expected space opened up for us. We then immediately tacked, both to get out of the backwind of boats dead ahead and
because we knew that the next leg was a very one-sided short beat, possibly
even a starboard fetch, to the finish (Figure 22). We were the second boat
to go about, and as it was indeed a fetch all the others lost whatever yard-
age they had sailed on the port tack. One other was able to sail over us because I had to pinch to lay the flag end; so we stole third, the best position
we had had all day.

Note that in Figure 22 the finish line was set square to the direction
of the last mark instead of square to the direction of the wind, even though
the leg was supposed to have been a beat to windward. Whether this is the
fairest way is open to question, but it is the way most committees set such
a finish line, so you might as well capitalize on it when you can. At least
two more boats would have beaten us that day had the line been across the
wind. After the finish I pointed out this piece of good luck to the crew, and
said, "As usual, the committee set a close-fetch finish square to the course.
The leeward end was favored by forty degrees. You can usually bet your
hat on this, or if you don't have a hat, anything else that comes handy."

It so happens that I would have lost that handy object had I bet it

**Figure 22**

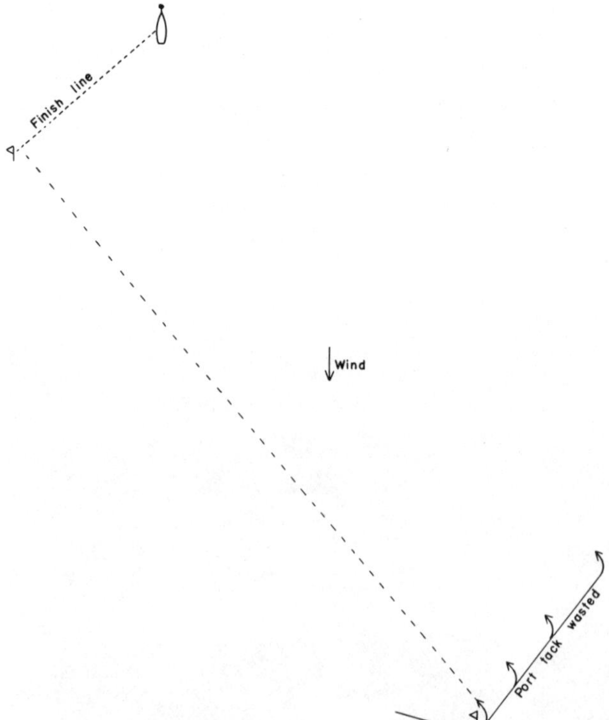

the following weekend. With the identical kind of last leg coming up we arrived at the leeward mark a close third behind Bill Ketcham. He expected me to try to round up and tack inside him, so he took the correct preventive action by tacking around the mark himself. This move put his boat on starboard tack, neatly in our way, and left us no alternative but to go around his stern and stand on for a few supposedly wasted yards on the port tack in order to get clear while he was sailing happily toward the finish on starboard. When we came about it looked as if we were both laying the finish and he would beat us by being at the favored (leeward) end. But this time the line was *very short* and *square to the wind,* two excellent attributes for any windward finish in my opinion. It was no coincidence that this race was being run by a small club that specializes in sail (no power boats), and whose chairman always does a superlative job. Needless to say, he is a racing skipper of considerable ability. We got a slightly favorable slant, or something; whatever it was, Bill had to tack for the finish, and we had him when we came together by virtue of being on starboard.

Although it has little to do with leeward marks, here is a hint to remember about finish lines in general. Many modern courses, whether quadrilateral or whatever, have a windward finish at the starting position. That is, a mark is set to leeward of the starting line and the committee boat simply stays on station, the last leg being a beat up to the finish. Some committees do not even bother to move the starting line at all. Others, if they shorten it for the finish, usually draw the flag straight in toward the committee boat without changing its bearing. You can see what this means: if the flag end was upwind at the start it will be upwind at the finish, and you should therefore finish at the committee end. In general, lacking any other indications, try to finish at what was the wrong end at the start. More often than not it is the right end at the finish. It is next to impossible, when beating up to a finish line, to tell which is the near end. The above determinative is better than a sheer guess.

# [II]
# SAILS

Sails have been in use for thousands of years, but racing sails for small yachts are a new concept. As recently as eighty years ago yacht sails were cut with the panels parallel to the leech, and carried no battens. The America's Cup yachts of 1930 used triple-head rigs instead of genoa jibs. The best sails were made of cotton until 1950. The making of small racing sails out of synthetic material is truly in its infancy. The only remark that can safely be made about the state of the art is that we hardly know what we are talking about. Skippers and sailmakers are still groping, feeling their way, progressing slowly by trial and error. There are plenty of fancy theories to choose from; but in the last analysis a sail is good if it wins races and not good if it loses races, and very little more can be said. To be sure, a poor sail can often be improved by a knowledgeable sailmaker, because he knows what to look for. When certain characteristics are missing he can sometimes supply or restore them by making suitable changes. But *why* these characteristics have to be there he is usually at a loss to say. We hear a lot about the slot, the twist, the location of the draft, and the like; but the real down-to-earth reasons, backed by physical theory, are hard to come by. Meanwhile we must plod along doing the best we can with the best sails available, which usually means those in use by the boats that are winning in your fleet. They may not be any faster than any other sailmaker's sails; but at least they are not *slower,* so in that sense they are a safe bet. I confess that I am not one to take a flier on a new sail from an untried source. The chances of hitting a right combination are slim. The people who know the most about your problems are the people who have been studying them. A sailmaker who makes championship sails for another class needs some practice (trial and error) before he can make them for yours. That is what I mean when I say that we don't really have the theory down yet; we must rely on the practice.

When synthetic material, notably Dacron, replaced cotton it was at first hailed as an economic boon. Here was a material much stronger than cotton, with far less stretch; why shouldn't a suit of sails last for years? Alas, the dream was quickly shattered: Dacron sails have a shorter winning life than cotton sails had. They do hold their shape—and yet they slow down. It took the sailmakers a long time to admit this. They have only recently come around to the view, long held by many racing people, that a Dacron sail is at its very best the day it is delivered and is never quite that fast again. It just slowly and imperceptibly goes downhill until one day you realize that you are racing with a slow sail that used to be a fast one. The sail may look just as good as ever. It hasn't lost its shape. Then what has it lost? The only possible explanation is that it has lost its *surface,* that fine glossy finish it had the day it came out of the bag. It has lost that finish by acquiring wrinkles and creases. Every bend and crack in the calendered finish means that much lost in the smoothness of the surface.

The other day a sailmaker told me of a mainsail he had made for a small keel boat. The owner was delighted with it; the boat was obviously faster. But this burst of speed didn't last. *One month later* the owner brought the sail back to the loft to ask what had happened to it. It was jammed into the bag like a spinnaker. "Yes, we always bag it that way. Is there some other way?" The sail was so badly wrinkled that in one month the surface had been permanently ruined.

Sailmakers recommend careful folding of the sails with the creases in a horizontal direction (parallel to the major airflow). The latest anti-

"Maxi masthead spinnakers" on Class A Scows. V-1's is supposed to be masthead too, but is fouled on the jumper.

LARSON

wrinkle device is the sausage-roll, practical for working jibs and small mainsails. The sail is rolled up around the foot and carried in a long tube-like bag requiring no folds at all, in order to delay as long as possible the onset of the wrinkles.

I have tried to beat the rap by starting with sailcloth that is softer to begin with, impregnated with little or no stabilizing resin. If it couldn't acquire creases, I thought, maybe it would last longer. The idea worked to some extent. The mainsail made with softer cloth was not spectacularly fast, but on the other hand it apparently held its initial performance level about twice as long as the stiffer sails. It seems a great waste to replace a fine Dacron sail, that ought to last almost indefinitely, after only one summer's use. Perhaps the next great advance in sailcloth will be a non-cracking finish that also has the desired gloss.

If a supersmooth surface is important—and everybody has to admit that it is—then we ought not to forget the stitching. Compared to the rest of the sail, the stitching at each seam is very rough. I don't know what to do about it but I'd like to be able to do something. For just that reason the numbers and insignia were not sewn but glued to our last mainsail—fine, until they all blew away one breezy day. There must be a better way.

A material characteristic that concerns some people is porosity. How much air escapes through the sailcloth? Obviously none through a six-ounce resin-impregnated working sail; but what about spinnakers? It is my belief that you might as well stop worrying about it. A spinnaker is often in a stalled-out attitude anyway, meaning that most of the air is blowing out around the edges. It would do no harm to have some excess air escaping through the sail. But the principal reason for my lack of concern is the exceedingly small percentage of air that does leak through so-called "porous" sailcloth. Engineering tests at air pressures much higher than those experienced on boats show little loss through porosity; and the amount of loss at normally experienced sailboat speeds is negligible.

In many one-design classes a strong effort is made to keep hull, spars, and rigging as strictly uniform as possible. When this is done the sails are the one big remaining variable. Take care of your sails, nurse them along, try to understand what they are doing for you. No one has sails down to a science. You have to learn by experience and by close observation of other boats. Why is he faster? What is he doing that I'm not doing? Probably a lot of things; but is there anything about his *sails* that I haven't noticed?

One of the prominent younger sailmakers, who was much involved with more than one of the 1974 America's Cup candidates, has suggested that not enough emphasis was placed on sail research and development in the early stages of the program. Every sailmaker worth his salt is a strong believer in the importance of his product; but discounting professional bias, there still may be something in the thought that a few new sails tried out on existing Twelve Meters in 1973 might have considerably advanced the chances of any one of the boats in the hectic trials of 1974. That was not done, and one season is too short a time to test new models and develop them to the point of peak performance.

Leaving out of consideration the specially designed reachers, what kind of shape characterizes a good spinnaker? Let us assume that your class rules or local racing conditions or both do not permit a wide choice, and that you are looking for an all-purpose running spinnaker that also has to carry you on a reach when necessary. Masthead spinnakers on big ocean racers are so much taller than they are wide that the construction methods are somewhat limited by the proportions. We are more concerned here with smaller spinnakers of lower aspect-ratio. What should you expect to see in a good sail of this type?

One school of thought favors a spinnaker with so-called high shoulders. By this is meant a sail that is full and high-riding in its upper portions. Is that good? Well, yes and no. Some of us have become disenchanted with high-shouldered spinnakers in recent years, for what is always the only unarguable reason: sails of another type are faster—sometimes. The reason that there is no one perfect spinnaker is clear enough: we are asking the same sail to do too many different things.

The high-shouldered spinnaker has a flat top or "roof" on it that at first glance seems wasted. Horizontal sailcloth is not projecting any area at right angles to the direction of the wind. But this roof serves a useful purpose. The wind flowing past the top of the sail creates an area of low pressure immediately ahead of and above the spinnaker, just as, in sailing to windward, low pressure is created behind the mainsail by the air from the jib. This low pressure generates a force with two useful components, a forward component that helps drive the boat, and an upward component that fills the head of the spinnaker and pulls all the rest of the sail into shape. Such a sail, then, ought to be and is at its best in rather light conditions dead before the wind. Unfortunately we no longer sail dead before the wind in light conditions, which is one reason the high-shouldered spinnaker is losing favor. Most people now look for a sail that is less deep, more plate-shaped than bowl-shaped. This flatter sail can be made to present a greater projected area to the wind on a run, and at the same time is a superior reaching sail. Looking from directly ahead at a boat running with the wind well abaft the beam, what I want to see is a spinnaker with a circular outline that flies high in any respectable strength of breeze. Such sails are available; get one if you can.

Spinnakers are made of nylon, which has a lot of stretch but twice the strength of Dacron weight for weight. Therefore, unlike your Dacron working sails, a spinnaker may have to be broken in. It will definitely improve after a few races as the stretching under tension smooths out the uneven places. A new spinnaker may fly with a crease or pleat down the center line for a few races. That doesn't do much harm if it ultimately works

F. NAKAJIMA

Both 31 and 77 have "flabby foot," an ailment typical of spinnakers whose vertical middimension is longer than the luffs.

itself out and disappears. Something else may take its place, however. If the sail becomes sufficiently stretched across the foot, usually by tight sheeting on reaches, the cloth cannot recover and will hang loose in a big fold or skirt across the bottom of the whole sail. E-22 spinnakers are especially subject to this flabby foot because of a long dimension from head to middle of foot. Send it back to the sailmaker at the end of its first season explaining what has happened, and he can easily fix it.

Spinnakers have little stiffening in the cloth, are not subject to surface cracking, and can stand being stuffed into a box or bag every day. They survive rough treatment for something so flimsy, and they age not through roughening of the surface, like Dacron sails, but through loss of shape. A spinnaker treated with loving care will serve you well for several seasons. If you are lucky enough to have an all-purpose spinnaker that makes the boat go, save it as long as possible. Better to lose a race by dousing it than try to carry through a severe thundersquall that would probably blow it out and bring an end to its career. Don't kill the goose for the sake of one last golden egg.

# [I2]
# THE RULES

This chapter will make no attempt to survey the racing rules. Excellent books are available on the subject, which is far too complex to cover in a single chapter. Some of the yachting magazines devote a column each month to the analysis of some one rule or a decision on an appealed case. Reading these columns is a good way to sharpen your knowledge and keep you up to date. Many yachtsmen are not as well acquainted with the rules as they should be. As a matter of self-protection you should know your rights. In fairness to the other skippers you should know your wrongs, and drop out when you commit one.

The first and best rule is, Keep out of trouble. By giving away a few feet you may be able to avoid a jam that would cost you many yards, even if you were in the right. On the other hand it is impossible to avoid *all* jams, and sometimes it even pays to take a deliberate chance. Knowledge of the rules is essential when you have to make a sudden decision whether or not to dive into a tight position. You must evaluate the situation in the light of the risks, facing the fact that you may have to withdraw or be disqualified from the race. It is not enough to *think* that you have the right of way; the race committee may think otherwise. It is far pleasanter to sail home at once, with your colors proudly flying, than to be tossed out unceremoniously three days later; and it has the same effect on the score.

I will mention only a few special and interesting cases, some of which occur often but are still not thoroughly understood. The first has to do with establishing an overlap at a leeward mark.

Under the old international rules (in force until 1965), an inside overlap had to be established "before the yacht clear ahead

STAN WESSEL BROADCASTING PHOTOGRAPHY, DALLAS

It looks very much as if the tiller of No. 24 is being pushed down too soon. She is too close to tack across No. 34's bow. She must give room for No. 34 *and her spinnaker pole* to fit through.

alters her course in the act of rounding." The act of rounding was usually considered to begin with the first alteration of course as the mark was being approached. This made it hard to establish the facts when the two boats were widely separated laterally, and many difficult protests resulted.

The current rules say nothing about the act of rounding. The proximity of the mark is defined in an altogether different way, by means of a circle with center at the mark and radius equal to two boat lengths of the leading boat. An overlap is clearly defined even when the two boats are far apart and sailing different courses. The outside boat must give room if the overlap exists while she is still outside the two-boat-length circle and about to enter that circle. Figure 23 depicts a state of affairs that develops in almost every race. At position 1, boat *B* is easily clear ahead of boat *A;* but now *B*'s spinnaker comes down and she goes for the mark on a beam reach. Suddenly *A* has acquired an overlap: if at position 2 any part of boat *A* is forward of "an imaginary line projected abeam from the aftermost point" of *B,* then *A* is entitled to room. Partly to counteract any lingering memories of the old rule, it is well for *A* to open negotiations immediately after *B* has made her turn, so as not to take her by surprise at position 2. If *B* refuses room on the grounds that she has already reached the circle, *A* should immediately bear off around *B*'s stern, and protest if she thinks fit. If *A* delays even for a second it will be too late for her to bear off and she will have to round up on the wrong side of the mark, a costly maneuver. There is always difference of opinion as to exactly when the two-length circle was reached, and *A* must remember that the burden of proof is on her to show that the overlap existed outside the circle.

This situation developed in the middle of and in addition to the incident described in Chapter 10 (Figure 22). As we neared the mark on a beam reach there was suddenly a seventh boat, aiming straight at us with an overlap. She was nowhere near overlapped when we started our turn for the mark; but we were still turning as we moved into the two-length circle, and whether the overlap was established in time I simply do not know. The burden of proof being on the other skipper, I brazenly shouted "No!" with a fleeting vision of at least three boats piled up in a mammoth wreck, and he turned out around our stern, doubtless unwilling to create the chaos that would have resulted had he tried to cut in.

The problem is aggravated when a group of boats arrives at the mark

**Figure 23**

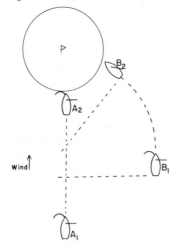

**US 41 did not have an overlap in time.**

in a line overlapped across the course. It is now impossible for the outside boats of the leading group to reach the two-length circle ahead of a boat coming in from another direction, or even from the same direction clear astern. Boat *A* in Figure 24 has an inside overlap on boats *D* and *E*. There have been those who thought this rule unfair, that *D* and *E* had won the race to the mark and should be entitled to rounding rights. Ted Wells, who is a member of the USYRU Racing Rules Committee, has responded in his usual incisive fashion:

> "As to 'winning the race to the mark,' the outer yachts in the front line have won the wrong race. If they are heading downwind for a finish line, they might be considered to have won, but this race is to get around a mark and five or six lengths laterally from the mark is no way to win the race to round the mark."

**Figure 24**

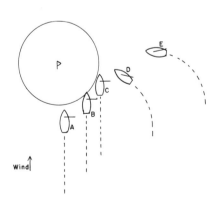

DIANE FEER

There seems to be no way that No. 3175 can avoid disqualification: No. 3407 has a whole boat length of overlap. No. 3647 may have been in the lead, but she has "lost the race to the mark."

The next case is one that you should be aware of lest you be tossed out of an important race by an alert competitor or committee. Suppose your bow is over the starting line too soon at the flag end, and in your efforts to delay till gunfire you also hit the flag—a fairly common occurrence. Most skippers seem to think it is enough to re-round the flag once and take off. Not so: you would have had to do that if you had *either* hit the flag *or* been over too soon. Since you did both, you have two penalties to pay. You must come around the flag once (or return some other way) to re-cross for being recalled, and then round once more for having touched the mark. (Authority: Case 42, IYRU Interpretations.)

The following questions are answered in Case 64 of the Royal Yachting Association, the top British rules authority.

"1. How many roundings does a yacht have to complete when she touches a mark on the first rounding? and

"2. How many roundings if she again touches the mark when attempting to re-round?

"Put diagrammatically, the question is, are the courses shown in Diagrams A and B [of Figure 25] the correct ones in their respective cases?

"*Answer:*

"1. In diagram A, the yacht having touched the mark on the far side in rounding it, Rule 52.1 required her to complete that rounding as required by the sailing instructions to sail the course. Thereafter, as a penalty, she was required to make an additional rounding of the mark without touching it. The diagram shows three roundings when two only were necessary.

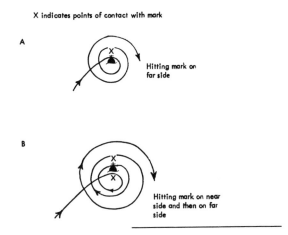

**Figure 25**

"2. In diagram B, the yacht having touched the mark on the near side was required to round it as required by the sailing instructions to sail the course. . . . Before she completed the first rounding of the mark as required to sail the course, she touched it again. Having completed this first rounding, as a penalty, she was required to make an additional rounding of the mark without touching it. The diagram shows three roundings when two only were necessary."

Don't forget that *while you are re-rounding* you have absolutely no rights (Rule 45.1).

Another one. You are winning the race in a very light wind against a slight tide. Though barely moving, you finally inch up to the line and get the finishing gun for first place. You relax, and sit there for a while, until the other boats begin to come along. Perhaps you think it would be a good idea to get out the paddle and move off the line? *No,* it would be a very bad idea. You are disqualified for doing this if you have failed to clear the line first; that is, all parts of the boat must have crossed. The first rule in the books says, "A yacht is racing . . . until she has . . . finished and cleared the finishing line."

On the other hand, once you have properly cleared the line you are safe. The boat in Figure 26 was carried into the finish-line flag by the tide and was disqualified by the race committee, but on appeal to the NAYRU she was exonerated.

"The intent of including 'finishing marks' as one of the criteria in determining when a yacht is no longer racing is to prevent a yacht which finishes so close to a mark that she is unable to avoid touching it from escaping penalty through the circumstance of having cleared the line

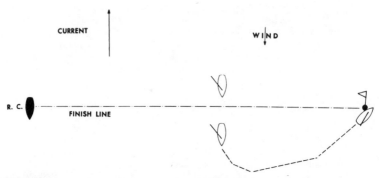

**Figure 26**

at the time of touching. The official diagram showed the yacht in this case to be some six lengths from the mark which she subsequently touched, so that at the time she cleared the line she was well clear of the mark. Her contact with the mark was no part of her finishing maneuver. It was, therefore, a separate incident, occurring when the yacht was no longer racing" (Appeal No. 136, 1970).

These are only a few of the special cases. All of the appeals make interesting and instructive reading. It is a lot more entertaining to study the peculiar predicaments that boats get themselves into than to get into them yourself.

The definition of a mark is "any object specified in the sailing instructions which a yacht must round or pass on a required side." Many race circulars contain the statement, "Government marks and aids to navigation must be passed on the channel side." Thus all government marks become marks of the course unless specifically exempted elsewhere in the instructions.

Touching a government mark may create an anomalous situation. Suppose you are racing around triangle *ABC* in Figure 27, leaving marks to port, and *G* is a government mark that must be passed on the side away from the shore. You are hugging the land as closely as possible to avoid an adverse current, and your spinnaker brushes *G* as you pass it on the correct side. You have now touched a mark of the course: "A mark has a required side for a yacht as long as she is on a leg which it begins, bounds or ends" (Rule 51.3). You may exonerate yourself only "by completing one entire rounding of the mark, leaving it on the required side," and then proceeding on your way (52.2(a)).

The difficulty is this. The required side of an ordinary mark of the course is either port or starboard; the required side of a government mark is the channel side. Therefore it is physically impossible to circle a government mark while leaving it always on the proper hand. You have to break one rule in order to conform with another.

It is not hard to see how this discrepancy arose. Prior to 1969 a yacht touching a mark without extenuating circumstances was automatically disqualified. The re-rounding rule, added that year, fits into some but not all of the previously existing wording. It would seem to be a matter of common sense that you could exonerate yourself by "re-rounding" a touched government mark (which you were never supposed to "round" in the first place), even though to do so you have to pass it once on the non-channel side. The case has not, to my knowledge, been ruled upon.

The following invention should qualify as the ultimate joke on the rule makers.

Suppose that the race circular specifies that the marks shall be left on the same hand as the starting flag, and that the race committee makes a mistake (it has been done), and sets the starting line with the flag to port for a course "Start-A-B-Finish" in Figure 28. Racing rule 51.2 reads: "A yacht shall sail the course so as to round or pass each mark on the required side in correct sequence, and so that a string representing her wake from the time she starts until she finishes would, when drawn taut, lie on the required side of each mark." The conventional way to comply with this rule under the stated circumstances is to sail the course shown in Figure 28, looping each mark so as to leave it to port. It is messy, and some of the boats do it wrong; but those who leave the mark to starboard are subject to disqualification.

The joke is this: Why couldn't a boat cross the starting line, sail once around the committee boat, crossing the starting line again, then turn and come back across the line a third time "from the direction of the last mark," and claim the race? The wording of the rule would in every respect have been fulfilled. Nowhere does any rule specify *how close* you have to pass a mark, provided it is on the required side.

I think that this is one that escaped the rule makers. But don't try it; it won't work. The NAYRU has already set a precedent by disqualifying a boat that took a shortcut across the course on a similar pretext. The decision reads, in part: "A rounding mark must be rounded; otherwise the minimum distance to be sailed, which it is the function of rounding marks to establish, is not fulfilled" (Appeal No. 155, 1973). They made this up out of whole cloth, because it was the only way they could avoid awarding the race to a skipper who sailed the course as shown in Figure 29. He claimed that by leaving *A* to port on the way to *B,* he had sailed the course "Start-A-B-Finish" leaving all marks on the proper hand. The district appeals committee upheld this claim, but the final authority of the North American Yacht Racing Union did not.

The famous photo on page 116 was taken by Edwin Levick at the start of a race of Larchmont Race Week on Wednesday, July 22, 1925. The boats are New York Forties, 59 feet on deck and about 75 feet from bowsprit tip to the end of the main boom. The starting line is between the dory in the lower lefthand corner and a flag on the committee boat con-

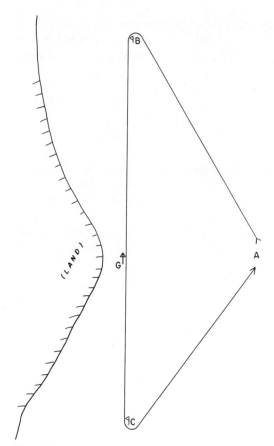

**Figure 27**

cealed by No. 8 (farthest left). The committee boat's white mooring can is visible under No. 8's bowsprit, and the after part of the boat, with a launch secured astern, can be seen under No. 46's mainsail.

Evidently the starting gun has not yet been fired. One would like to know how much time remains and what is going to happen next, but that information is probably lost forever. A foul did occur, but not the one you think. Harry Maxwell's *Banshee,* No. 8, sailed by a man named Johnson, fouled Joseph Dunbaugh's *Shawara,* No. 40, the boat astern and to leeward. The report in the *New York Times* of July 23, 1925, states:

> "It was hard for the skippers to hold the Forties with the breeze roaring along at 35 knots, and while trying to keep his big sloop from crossing the line before the gun Captain Johnson bore down on *Shawara, Banshee's* backstay catching the Dunbaugh sloop's boom. *Banshee* sailed a fine race and was almost a minute and a half ahead of

Holland Duell's *Rowdy* after a hard battle in the rough seas. The committee was compelled to disqualify the Maxwell sloop because of the unintentional foul, the race going to *Rowdy,* with *Mistral* placing second."

The first sentence contains an obvious error: the words *boom* and *backstay* should be interchanged. More interesting, however, is the journalist's bias in describing the "unintentional" foul. Is any foul intentional? *"Banshee* sailed a fine race"; yes, with the aid of an illegal maneuver that saved her from being recalled and robbed *Shawara* of a perfectly timed and executed start. The reporter implies a definite reluctance on the part of the committee to toss out the offender, whether such reluctance did in fact exist or not. It is this sort of editorializing that has helped to give protesting the bad name that has often dogged it.

The foul could hardly have occurred before the picture was taken, because No. 40, with full way, is considerably astern of No. 8, whose sails are half aback and is therefore traveling more slowly than No. 40. Probably No. 8 is about to bear off to return to the right side of the line; in doing so she finds No. 40 close aboard to leeward, her people shouting for their rights, and the contact occurs.

You may wonder why *Rowdy,* the leeward of the two boats in the foreground, does not luff *Mistral,* No. 46, over the line (if indeed she is not over already). The reason is that the luffing rights of a leeward boat before the start were more severely restricted by the racing rules of half a century ago than they are today. Everything depended on how they got into position. The relative mast heights show that the leeward boat is far-

**Figure 28**

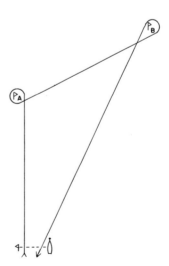

EDWIN LEVICK

**New York Forties in a squall.**

ther from the camera than the weather boat. She may rank as overtaking and have no rights. In any event No. 46 got away with it and was credited with a clear start.

The wind strength was perhaps subject to the conventional exaggeration. Twenty-four Stars started and they all finished without mishap. Nevertheless it was "a hard southwest blow, accompanied by frequent heavy rain squalls." The sky at starting time was not so black as this picture would

**Figure 29**

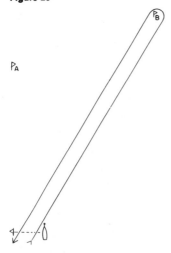

have it. Mr. Levick experimented with various versions, and there exist other copies showing a much brighter sky; but all have the same rough water.

If you fancy yourself a rules expert, see whether you can pass this stiff test: Write down all the *exceptions* to the rule, "Starboard tack has the right of way." There are at least fifteen such exceptions. If you don't believe it, check carefully racing rules 32, 34, 35, 41.2, 41.4, 42.1(a)(ii), 42.1(b)(i), 42.2(a)(i), 43, 44, 45, 46, and 67.

# [13]
# THE COX-SPRAGUE SCORING SYSTEM

The approved scoring system of the Yacht Racing Association of Long Island Sound has for many years been the Cox-Sprague system. How widely it has been adopted elsewhere I do not know. As recorder for a YRA fleet I have become well acquainted with the system, and I would like to commend it to your attention if your racing circumstances are at all similar to ours.

A number of years ago, when William S. Cox was one of several keen skippers racing in the hotly contested International One Design fleet on Long Island Sound, he and Henry Sprague became interested in devising a "best possible" scoring method. They discovered that at least sixteen different scoring systems were then in use in the U.S.A., and that all of them incorporated, to a greater or lesser degree, each of the following inequities:

1. Unrealistic award of points in any one race.
2. Incorrect weighting of the size of a race.
3. Disregard of the disastrous effect of a d.n.f. (did not finish).

Cox and Sprague produced a system that minimizes all of these defects.

The Cox-Sprague system was invented for, and works best in, a long series of races such as an all-summer championship in which each boat is allowed a high percentage of absenteeism. In our class today, for instance, one can qualify by sailing in only half of the thirty-five scheduled races. In a short series where everyone expects to participate in every race, the difficulty number 2 does not arise, and number 3 can be avoided by a worst-race exemption. But in the season-long championship, all three difficulties present themselves; and there are many such series in progress throughout the country every summer. It is for them that the system displays its greatest merits. Let us take the three points in order.

1. What is meant by a realistic distribution of point awards in any one race? The theoretical assumption is that the points gained should be somehow proportional to the difficulty of earning them. This is easier said than decreed. But at least it is easy to see what is *not* realistic, one example being the linear system in which, if 20 boats start, 20 points are awarded for first, 19 for second, and so on down. The linear scheme implies that it is no more difficult to move from fifteenth to fourteenth, for instance, than it is to move from second to first. Anyone who has ever started last and had to claw his way up through the fleet knows very well that this just isn't so. As you work upward the going gets progressively rougher, and it takes much talent or lots of luck to go from second to first. The difference in score between first and second ought therefore to be greater than the difference in score between fourteenth and fifteenth. The point awards should lie not on a straight line but along a curve that steepens near the top.

The old Olympic scoring system took care of this in a drastic way by distributing the points on an exponential, or logarithmic, curve. The difference in points between first and second was the same as that between second and fourth, and the same as that between tenth and twentieth. It was finally decided that this was too steep a curve, and in 1968 a milder point graduation was instituted.

The Cox-Sprague system is based on a curve that says, in effect, that to move from second place to first place in a race is worth twice as much as to move from fifth place to fourth, and three times as much as to move from tenth to ninth. The differences between any two adjacent figures in the vertical columns of the table yield these comparisons. If the figures in any one column, say the one marked "20 or more," are plotted against a set of intervals spaced evenly from 1 to 20, they lie approximately along a smooth curve. The original version of the system had a more formidable table with everything carried to one more decimal place, in order to fit the figures more closely to the curve. Rounding to only two decimal places introduces a kink or bend in the curve at thirteenth place; in fact it consists of a straight line from sixth to thirteenth and then another straight line from thirteenth on down.

It is interesting to note that the current Olympic system, when plotted on the same scale, follows quite closely the Cox-Sprague curve. Whether or not this was by design I do not know.

It is undoubtedly more difficult to move from second to first than it is to move from third to second. Whether it is exactly 1.5 times as difficult (simplified Cox-Sprague), or 1.1 times as difficult (Olympic), or 1.7 times as difficult (old Olympic), who can say? The point is that *some* difficulty factor should be built into the system, and the Cox-Sprague has features soon to be mentioned that indicate that Messrs. Cox and Sprague hit on a meaningful and practicable curve.

They are doing things in the right sequence: get the man back on the boat first, and worry about the mess later.

2. A boat's score for one race is obtained by dividing the points earned by the possible points. If for instance there were 18 starters and you finished third, the column headed 18 shows that your score for that day was 88/98, or .898. This is almost as good as a third with 20 boats (.900) and much better than a third with 4 boats (.767). What is more important, however, is that the running score is kept not by averaging the points for each day (which would equally weight all races), but by totaling all the points you have so far for the season and dividing that total by the sum of all the possible points for the races in which you sailed. In short, a running fraction is maintained, so that after each race new points are added to the numerator and to the denominator and the resulting new fraction is your score to date. This procedure is what gives less weight to the smaller races.

Suppose two boats are fighting for series top honors, as so often happens. On Saturday $A$ finishes first and $B$ second, in a race with 20 boats. The next day is cold and stormy and only 10 show up, but of course $A$ and $B$ are out there hammer and tongs; and this time they trade places. It would not seem fair to penalize $B$ because she happened to get her first in

## COX-SPRAGUE SCORING SYSTEM

| No. of Starters 2 | 3 | 4 | 5 | 6 | 7 | 8 | 9 | 10 | 11 | 12 | 13 | 14 | 15 | 16 | 17 | 18 | 19 | 20 or More | Place |
|---|---|---|---|---|---|---|---|---|---|---|---|---|---|---|---|---|---|---|---|
| 10 | 31 | 43 | 52 | 60 | 66 | 72 | 76 | 80 | 84 | 87 | 90 | 92 | 94 | 96 | 97 | 98 | 99 | 100 | 1 |
| 4 | 25 | 37 | 46 | 54 | 60 | 66 | 70 | 74 | 78 | 81 | 84 | 86 | 88 | 90 | 91 | 92 | 93 | 94 | 2 |
| (0) | 21 | 33 | 42 | 50 | 56 | 62 | 66 | 70 | 74 | 77 | 80 | 82 | 84 | 86 | 87 | 88 | 89 | 90 | 3 |
| | (17) | 29 | 38 | 46 | 52 | 58 | 62 | 66 | 70 | 73 | 76 | 78 | 80 | 82 | 83 | 84 | 85 | 86 | 4 |
| | | (26) | 35 | 43 | 49 | 55 | 59 | 63 | 67 | 70 | 73 | 75 | 77 | 79 | 80 | 81 | 82 | 83 | 5 |
| | | | (32) | 40 | 46 | 52 | 56 | 60 | 64 | 67 | 70 | 72 | 74 | 76 | 77 | 78 | 79 | 80 | 6 |
| | | | | (38) | 44 | 50 | 54 | 58 | 62 | 65 | 68 | 70 | 72 | 74 | 75 | 76 | 77 | 78 | 7 |
| | | | | | (42) | 48 | 52 | 56 | 60 | 63 | 66 | 68 | 70 | 72 | 73 | 74 | 75 | 76 | 8 |
| | | | | | | (46) | 50 | 54 | 58 | 61 | 64 | 66 | 68 | 70 | 71 | 72 | 73 | 74 | 9 |
| | | | | | | | (48) | 52 | 56 | 59 | 62 | 64 | 66 | 68 | 69 | 70 | 71 | 72 | 10 |
| | | | | | | | | (50) | 54 | 57 | 60 | 62 | 64 | 66 | 67 | 68 | 69 | 70 | 11 |
| | | | | | | | | | (52) | 55 | 58 | 60 | 62 | 64 | 65 | 66 | 67 | 68 | 12 |
| | | | | | | | | | | (53) | 56 | 58 | 60 | 62 | 63 | 64 | 65 | 66 | 13 |
| | | | | | | | | | | | (55) | 57 | 59 | 61 | 62 | 63 | 64 | 65 | 14 |
| | | | | | | | | | | | | (56) | 58 | 60 | 61 | 62 | 63 | 64 | 15 |
| | | | | | | | | | | | | | (57) | 59 | 60 | 61 | 62 | 63 | 16 |
| | | | | | | | | | | | | | | (58) | 59 | 60 | 61 | 62 | 17 |
| | | | | | | | | | | | | | | | -(58) | 59 | 60 | 61 | 18 |
| | | | | | | | | | | | | | | | | (58) | 59 | 60 | 19 |
| | | | | | | | | | | | | | | | | | (58) | 59 | 20 |

Pts in ( ) are for DNF & Disq.

| Place | Pts. | Place | Pts. | Place | Pts. |
|---|---|---|---|---|---|
| 21 | 58 | 31 | 48 | 41 | 38 |
| 22 | 57 | 32 | 47 | 42 | 37 |
| 23 | 56 | 33 | 46 | 43 | 36 |
| 24 | 55 | 34 | 45 | etc. | etc. |
| 25 | 54 | 35 | 44 | | |
| 26 | 53 | 36 | 43 | | |
| 27 | 52 | 37 | 42 | | |
| 28 | 51 | 38 | 41 | | |
| 29 | 50 | 39 | 40 | | |
| 30 | 49 | 40 | 39 | | |

the smaller race. In this case, the size of the race didn't really matter: it was equally difficult for *B* to beat *A* no matter how many boats were out. The system takes care of this by maintaining the same point differentials between positions. The two boats would indeed conclude the weekend with no change in their relative positions. Their total fractions would be higher, but by the same amounts. Among all boats that enter the same races, the size-of-race factor is almost nullified. It is of more consequence to the boats that stayed home. Against boats that are not out there at all, the leaders in a big race raise their total score more than the leaders in a little race.

3. Under traditional scoring systems a disqualification, or withdrawal due to breakdown or whatever cause, can put a boat out of contention for the series. Some skippers (of the old guard?) think that this is as it should be; but the trend today is in the direction of milder penalties. The IYRU is suggesting options other than total disqualification, such as the 360° or 720° turn. This is a can of worms that I would prefer not to open; current discussions on the subject tend to become overheated. Perhaps some day we will have graduated penalties, perhaps not. In any event, if someone travels halfway around the world to participate in an international championship, it does seem harsh to deprive him of all chance of winning because of a mishap in the opening race. To counter this disaster many such

championships are now sailed with a worst-race exemption, each competitor being allowed to discard his worst race before compiling his total series score.

The Cox-Sprague system meets the problem differently, by making the penalty less severe to start with. A d.n.f. costs in the neighborhood of $58/100$, and not $0/100$ as it would in a straight linear system. This penalty is stiff but not calamitous. It does not ruin an entire season's efforts. An illustration of how it affects the score was provided by last summer's Labor Day weekend of three races that were all part of our season championship. The leading boat, a little off the pace for some reason, had a respectable but undistinguished 4-7-6. The second boat turned in a withdrew-1-4. All the races had 20 or more entries, and a glance at the table shows that 7-6 exactly balances dnf-1, both totaling 158 points. Far from being knocked out irrevocably, the boat that had had to withdraw for a foul was in no worse shape vis-à-vis the leader than before the weekend began. This was of course partly due to the quite substantial bonus that the system awards to first place.

In our fleet we tried a worst-race exemption for one season, but dropped it the following year because with the Cox-Sprague system it seemed unnecessary and not worth the trouble. A worst-race exemption has the great disadvantage of making everyone's score uncertain up to the last race: there is no way of knowing in advance which race is going to be the discarded one. Each score has to be figured twice, first discarding the worst race to date and again saving the discard against a potential worst race of the future. This fact requires special covering tactics toward the end of any closely contested series that includes such an exemption. I will not consider them here because they do not arise in the kind of racing that you and I are mainly concerned with.

Your fleet might want to introduce a worst-race exemption into its scoring system for a different reason: to encourage attendance. If you have a problem of boats not showing up once they have qualified, an added incentive might be to allow one or more exemptions to all boats sailing X number of additional races after qualification. The Cox-Sprague scoring system admittedly has no such incentive built into it. But the need seems to be minimal. With very few exceptions most skippers, especially the top ones, enjoy racing so much that they keep on coming out after qualifying without too much regard for protecting their scores. Let it be anyone's privilege to stop if he wants to; but it does seem rather a reversal of values to deprive oneself of racing in order to guarantee winning the series.

# [14]
# GETTING IT
# ALL TOGETHER

We have been covering considerable ground, going over a lot of details separately. The remaining question is how to assemble it all. How can you organize yourself for a better racing season?

One skipper in our fleet did it a couple of years ago. Very discouraged because of finishing the season at the bottom of the list, he made up his mind that he was going to do something about it. First he bought out his partner, in order to become the full-time skipper of the boat. Then he went to work and gave the boat a really good racing bottom for the first time. He read books. They taught him some things he didn't know, and reminded him of many things he had forgotten.

He made a point of having long talks during the winter with the best skippers in the fleet. If you do this on the basis of "I need all the help I can get; *anything* that you could tell me would be great," and then listen attentively, they will often open up. The good skippers are secretive only in front of the other good skippers. Give them a chance and they will generally spill their best beans.

He bought a new suit of the sails that seemed to be proving the most satisfactory to the greatest number of the class's skippers. He signed up a *regular, young* crew: two brothers who were not even connected with the yacht club, who were inexperiencd but eager, and who had no boat of their own, a good combination.

He took his racing seriously, giving it the No. 1 priority for the summer, and did not let anything else get in its way. He even changed the name of the boat to something symbolizing "The sky's the limit."

The result of all this was spectacular. From dead last at the end of the previous season the boat became an ever-present contender near the top of the fleet. She took daily first, second, or third eight times, and finished seventh out of nineteen boats qualifying for the season's championship. The skipper and the boys had a summer they will never forget, and the fleet acquired a fine new competitor.

Any successful season involves some planning, some preparation, and a good deal of thought. The *Puff* syndicate is a prime example. *Puff* was a Ranger 33, bought new in the fall of 1970 by a group of four young men in their twenties and early thirties, all of whom already had creditable racing records. They knew one another well, and agreed in what they were doing and what they wanted to do. They set aside one evening per week to meet and work on the boat, and they kept this schedule faithfully all winter long, as well as contributing occasional weekend time. *Puff* was never far from their waking thoughts. They had bought the boat bare, and during the winter they collected and installed the hardware and other fittings that study and consultation had determined were the ones *they* wanted. Thus the whole boat was assembled from scratch to their liking, while at the same time they became thoroughly familiar with the purpose and location of every fitting, even of each nut and bolt. While working they plotted and planned the summer's campaign, and also ironed out how they were going to distribute responsibilities and duties while racing. Many syndicates are wrecked on the rocks of acrimony developed through misunderstanding and divided authority. This one was a true partnership with several skippers (helmsmen), that survived all storms by never allowing any to brew up. *Puff* was a straight stock boat, with only the optional fittings making her any different from her sisterships. But the whole approach was an unbeatable one and *Puff* had a whirlwind season, virtually sweeping the board in most of the events she entered in 1971.

Skipper-crew mutual confidence is assuredly a must. That is why it is so important to get and keep a steady crew. Too many skippers decide on Friday night that they are going to race this weekend after all. From that moment on, everything becomes a mad rush to get ready. A crew must be assembled, but by Friday night the good ones have all been signed up long ago. The chances of finding somebody capable at the club at the last minute are extremely small. I have heard skippers who operate this way complain that they "never seem to be able to get good crews." Of course not; how could they?

I try either to sign the same crew on from the summer before, or assemble a new one very early, perhaps in March or April, so that we can get together once or twice to talk about the coming season and sweep the winter cobwebs out of our heads. After that we can hardly wait for the racing to start. I have had better luck with enthusiastic youngsters than with people my age who become so involved with other responsibilities and commitments that they cannot possibly sail regularly. The youngsters keep coming back for more, and seem to get genuinely interested in the welfare and performance of the boat. Don't worry if you can't sign on a super crew at the outset: *you* are going to make them into that. And if you can get only one who looks potentially steady and faithful, let him produce another one or two from among his friends. They will work well together and will enjoy it much more than racing with strangers.

It is a mistake to ditch your all-summer crew in favor of some allegedly more experienced "experts" who might volunteer to sail with you in the year's major event, like a national championship or whatever. Your regulars have been looking forward to that series as much as you have. They qualified the boat to enter the series, and they deserve to sail in it. Besides, by the end of the season they are better than anyone else you could import, however famous. By now you are a team, you know each other well and operate together smoothly and efficiently. I, for one, do not sail as well as I should with a name skipper in the crew. I am too ready to listen to his advice, and unless a pair works together all summer, there can be only one captain. There is not time to consult on every decision, and if you are working on two different race plans at once you inevitably end up falling on your face somewhere between the two. A steady crew knows how much help you want and when to give it, you never annoy each other, and costly misunderstandings no longer occur.

There is a substantial amount of psychological momentum in a winning streak. When things get going just right they stay going for weeks on end. You expect to do well in every race and somehow you do. The boat is in the groove. Conversely, on the *Flame* at any rate, there are periods of relative gloom when nothing goes right. How or why this happens I do not know. If I did I might be able to tell you how to prevent it. I do know that once the skipper falls into a losing frame of mind, the damage has been done and is hard to repair. All the breaks go against you. Time after time you choose the wrong tack, until you begin to mistrust your speed and your judgment and everything else. Then you get desperate and take chances and sail in a generally sloppy fashion, which of course makes matters worse. Finally one day it dawns on you that all this has got to stop. You have a little talk with yourself. You get down to business and, with the aid of the ever faithful crew who have been quietly waiting out the storm, you put it all together again.

# [15]
# THE LAVISH SUMMER

"No price is set on the lavish summer"
JAMES RUSSELL LOWELL

This book opened in a low key. I said that I would try to provide you with some hints for the ordinary sailor, some methods, ideas, suggestions that you, as a serious racing skipper but no fanatic, might put to good use. Have I come even close to fulfilling that promise, or has the brew gradually been strengthened to a concentration not originally intended? At times the subject matter has been somewhat technical. I trust that it has never become too high powered.

It is easy to be carried away with enthusiasm, to be caught up in the atmosphere of excitement that surrounds a good race. There is nothing wrong with this, if it stops there. The danger is that intensity of involvement may get out of control. As soon as the importance of winning the race takes complete command, then the sun is blotted out, the black clouds descend, and before you know it you are wearing an angry scowl and can see no farther than the bow of the boat, if that far. If you lose the race the day has been lost, and you return to the mooring with a vile temper and a sullen crew.

That is not my idea of the way to spend an afternoon on the water. The lavish summer is all too short. The poet is trying to tell us that the best things in life are free. If a first place must be bought at the cost of mental turmoil and anguish that obliterate the surrounding scenery, then the price is too high. I would rather settle for a second or a third, earned pleasantly and in the relaxed (but not too relaxed!) atmosphere of good companionship, and with an occasional glance of appreciation at the blue sky and the sparkling sea. Besides, seconds and thirds often add up to a first in the series. You can have it both ways if you play it cool.

I once heard a man say, "I had to give up racing. My doctor advised me to stay ashore." But he was no happier ashore. Whatever was wrong had nothing to do with racing. I recommend the opposite treatment. I cannot remember ever having missed a race for reasons of health. I have raced with a cracked rib, with a sprained back, with malarial fever; I once sailed a major Star series with an arm in a sling. Always I felt better after the race than before it. Whenever there is anything wrong with me, a good race is generally the best cure.

If the goal is enjoyment of the race, you can't lose. This is the common tie that unites skipper and crew and makes a happy ship. George E. Hills, the American racing rules authority of a vanished generation, wrote of his own racing career, "When at Hingham we thought nothing of sailing eight or ten miles to some point in Boston Harbor to enter a race. Sometimes we won. Sometimes we lost. But we had a wonderful time." Of course they took the whole day to do this, and enjoyed every minute of it. One does not see enough of that going on today. The modern notion seems to be to sandwich the racing into a schedule already overcrowded with other activities. Sailing deserves more consideration than that. The race should be given a higher priority than mowing the lawn or attending a cocktail party.

Surely the trials for the selection of a defender for the America's Cup are about as serious a proposition as any in the whole of yacht racing. There could have been no more tightly fought contest than the campaign of the summer of 1974. Yet, to their everlasting credit, the *Intrepid* crew produced a quiet display of team work, integrity, and mutual confidence that outshone all the fanfare surrounding the other Twelves. Not to be selected in the end must have been a grievous disappointment; yet there was no trace of bitterness in the remarks of *Intrepid*'s skipper Gerald Driscoll: "It was the best summer of racing we had in our lives. We wouldn't trade places with anybody. We got everything but the frosting on the cake."

They had made the most of the lavish summer.

# INDEX